PENGUIN BOOKS

THE INSTANT GOURMET

Melissa Clark, a former caterer, resides in New York City, where she is a freelance writer. She earned her M.F.A. in writing from Columbia University and is currently working on a book based on interviews with New York City chefs. This is her third cookbook.

The
Instant
Gourmet

**Delicious Meals
in 20 Minutes or Less**

Melissa Clark

Produced by the Philip Lief Group, Inc.

Penguin Books

PENGUIN BOOKS
Published by the Penguin Group
Penguin Books USA Inc., 375 Hudson Street,
New York, New York 10014, U.S.A.
Penguin Books Ltd, 27 Wrights Lane,
London W8 5TZ, England
Penguin Books Australia Ltd, Ringwood,
Victoria, Australia
Penguin Books Canada Ltd, 10 Alcorn Avenue,
Toronto, Ontario, Canada M4V 3B2
Penguin Books (N.Z.) Ltd, 182–190 Wairau Road,
Auckland 10, New Zealand

Penguin Books Ltd, Registered Offices:
Harmondsworth, Middlesex, England

First published in Penguin Books 1995

10 9 8 7 6 5 4 3 2 1

The product names used in this book that are known to be trademarks appear in
initial capital letters (e.g., Goya).

ISBN 0 14 02.4140 X
(CIP data available)

Printed in the United States of America
Set in Bodoni Book
Designed by Linda Kocur

contents

sources

Dean & DeLuca
560 Broadway
New York NY 10012
(800) 227-7714

La Cuisine
323 Cameron Street
Alexandria, VA 22314
(800) 521-1176

Williams-Sonoma
Mail Order Department
P.O. Box 7456
San Francisco, CA 94120-7456
(415) 421-4242

Woodland Pantry
Forest Foods, Inc.
P.O. Box 373
River Forest, IL 60305

Zabar's Deli & Gourmet Foods
2245 Broadway
New York, NY 10036
(212) 787-2000

introduction

It seems so odd to be sitting at my computer at two in the morning, typing an introduction to a book that is completely finished. How does one even try to begin something that has already ended?

Rather than delve into the many answers to that question, I will instead write about the party I gave that just broke up. It was a combination house-warming and book-completion party, and of course, having had the double burden of unpacking a home and writing a book against a very tight deadline, I didn't have much—or, really, any—time to dedicate to a party.

So after all the dip is depleted, all the canapés consumed, I can say, with all sincerity and for purely selfish reasons, that it's a good thing I wrote this book. I cannot imagine how I would have pulled off a party without it.

The game plan was simple: I called up my close friend Ana Deboo and had her come over thirty minutes early to break the ends off the sugar snap peas I asked her to pick up on the way. Another friend, Robin Aronson, was on time (a rare thing at a party), and so was conscripted to slam the ice in the bathtub until it broke up into manageable pieces, and to put the bread and crackers out. The rest of the work I did myself. It consisted of making two dips, which took five minutes each, both made with staple pantry items. The Caesar dressing was for the romaine hearts I had purchased prewashed at a nearby salad bar, and the peanut dip was made with prepared peanut sauce and served with the sugar snap peas.

Then I arranged the cheeses on a handmade ceramic platter and drizzled each cheese with a different oil. The aged Gruyère was sprinkled with walnut oil and chopped toasted walnuts; the fresh mozzarella was doused with sun-dried tomatoes and the packing oil; and the fresh goat cheese was coated with chopped herbs from my window box and drizzled with fragrant olive oil.

I then unpacked the jewellike array of Indian and Pakistani sweets I had picked up at a local restaurant. These make a dramatic presentation, and you don't need to buy very many. Good olives were placed in glass bowls and decorated with lemon slices, and I unwrapped some coarse country pâté. The last dish was the only thing I had made in advance—the sun-dried tomato lavash rolls—because they slice so much better after they have been chilled. That was it, the whole party, and people were thrilled.

Of course, any party will be a success if you have the right mix of good talkers and keen listeners, and enough wine, but everyone kept raving about the food. Ridiculously easy, I thought.

"Oh, it was nothing," I said. I meant it, but no one believed me. This is the spirit of this book.

Enjoy and impress.

ingredients

Using the very finest ingredients is always one of the most important parts of good cooking. For this book, since the ingredients are so few, they must be pristine and full of flavor. This applied not only to fresh ingredients such as produce, meats, seafood, etc., but also to the prepared ingredients, such as the sauces and condiments used throughout the book. Below are some tips to finding and storing the ingredients used in the recipes.

Prepared Sauces: Much of this book depends upon good-quality prepared sauces for flavor. Pesto, peanut sauce, tomato sauce, and salsa are all relatively easy to find (or mail-order) and will make cooking an absolute snap for the time-pressed. What is important when using prepared products is to find the very best available. Let your palate, and not the cost of an item, be your guide.

If you have the time (and who really does?), I have offered a Basics chapter providing recipes for many of the prepared products listed in the book.

Sun-Dried Tomatoes: There are three ingredients I find myself using over and over. They are sun-dried tomatoes, pesto sauce, and olivada. The reasons are simple. They are relatively easy-to-procure, very flavorful products that are open to hundreds of variations. What more could a cook want? That they should be inexpensive too, but since this book deals with time-effectiveness and not cost-effectiveness, we won't worry about that.

Sun-dried tomatoes have become incredibly popular over the past five years, but just because they are ubiquitous does not mean that they should be ignored by the food-snob set. They still taste wonderfully pungent and alive. For the time-pressed cook, the oil-packed varieties are undeniably the best bet. They need no soaking and can therefore be added directly to any dish.

However, here are some tips for the parsimonious, or for those of you with the hard-as-leather dried kind in your cupboard. As my brilliant friend Amy Martin reminds me, the best and quickest way to plump up arid tomatoes is to put them in a colander and run boiling water over them. They will soften right up. If you happen to be making pasta with your sun-dried tomatoes, you can place the dried tomatoes in the bottom of your colander and empty the pasta over them. The boiling pasta water will soften them, and you can simply add some good olive oil and Parmesan cheese and have a feast.

Olivada: This smooth paste consists of either black or green olives, olive oil, and sometimes herbs and seasonings. It is a real boon for time-pressed cooking, since it tastes just wonderful merely smeared on a slice of toast as a cocktail nibble. Toss it with pasta or dab it on fish, and you have a hearty and flavorful sauce. Olivada is available at most specialty markets, especially Italian ones. You can also mail-order it from Dean & DeLuca (see Sources, page vi), or make your own (page 233).

Olives: Good-quality olives are the easiest things in the world to have for a party. Just place them in a pretty bowl, maybe mixing two or three different shapes and colors, and you will have a stunning and tasty mosaic for your guests. I frequently call for olives in this book, sometimes pitted and sometimes not. As a general rule, I try not to pit the olives unless I have some very fussy VIPs to entertain. Most of my guests are not so refined that they object to delicately discarding the pits. If you must pit, buy olives with crinkly, soft flesh that can easily be squeezed between your fingers.

Here's a tip I learned from one of Barbara Kafka's cookbooks for pitting a large number of olives at one time. Simply lay them all out on a baking sheet on a counter, then smash them with the bottom of a heavy pot. The olive flesh will break on impact and the pit will be easy to pick out. For small amounts of olives I just squish them between my fingers and pull out the pits.

Pesto: It is now incredibly easy to walk into any large supermarket and buy an excellent prepared pesto. Pesto freezes well if you are buying the refrigerated rather than the bottled kind, and is a good thing to have on hand for instant dinners.

Roasted Peppers and Marinated Artichoke Hearts: I have put these two very different ingredients under the same heading because they are used in similar ways. That is, they can be tossed into pastas or onto pizzas, chopped up and spread over fish and poultry, or made into a simple sauce for meats. They are good served plain in small glass bowls, and they make a divine sandwich filling.

However, for both these products you need to be mindful of quality. Although it is hard to recommend the best national brands, I can give some tips on choosing an excellent product, as we all know that price alone does not guarantee quality. The first is to buy your peppers and artichokes from a delicatessen specializing in Italian foods. If they have platters of prepared foods behind the counter that include these two items, then you will probably be able to taste them before you buy. If not, look for peppers and artichokes packed in extra-virgin olive oil. If the manufacturers bother with the expense of extra-virgin olive oil, then you know that they care about their product. Generally, as with all prepared foods, the fewer ingredients the better, and they should consist of things that you would use if you were preparing them yourself, like peppers, oil, salt, and lemon juice. Sugar and other sweeteners do not belong in either product but are unfortunately quite common in peppers. Brine-packed peppers are okay so long as they are roasted, peeled, and unsweetened.

Vegetables: Think salad bar whenever you consider using fresh vegetables in this book. Many salad bars have an excellent selection of sliced or cubed, washed, and ready-to-eat vegetables that are easy to throw into salads or sautés. Also, they have nice washed lettuces and watercress, not to mention the mesclun that is always sold table-ready.

Salad Dressings: Unfortunately, there are few decent, let alone excellent, salad dressings on the market today. A few exceptions are Spoon Food's Salad Dazzlers, which I think need some olive oil added, and the Silver Palate Caesar dressing, which has a wonderful kick from all the garlic and Parmesan cheese it contains. Otherwise, I advise making your own dressing once a week and storing it in the refrigerator. It is not quite as timeless as the prepared kind, but it will taste better.

Oil: Olive oil is my choice for most of the sautéing I do. Use the best-quality extra-virgin olive oil you can afford. Extra-virgin oil is derived from the first, "virgin" pressing of the olive. Sometimes the label will also read "cold-pressed" oil. This signifies a purer, better-quality oil. All extra-virgin oils are cold-pressed, but not all cold-pressed oils are extra-virgin, so read the label carefully. Colavita is a good, easily obtainable, and reasonably priced brand that I recommend for cooking. For salads and other raw uses, use an even more flavorful one, preferably imported from Italy, although France and even California are now producing excellent oils. I used to hold to the notion that the darker and murkier the oil, the stronger the flavor is likely to be. I have since been proved wrong on occasion, but I still believe it is a viable recommendation.

Nut oils are wonderful for both cooking and salad dressings. Hazelnut and walnut are the two I use in this book because they are the ones with the most flavor. I find almond oil too bland for anything other than a massage. Make sure to store nut oils in the refrigerator, as they will go rancid quickly if left at room temperature. If the oil congeals in the fridge, just let it sit at room temperature until you can pour it; then proceed with the recipe. If you don't have enough time to let it sit, then run the bottle under hot water. The oil will melt immediately.

For flavorless oils, use anything without saturated fat. This is for health reasons, not flavor. Corn oil will probably be cheaper than the highly touted canola oil, and it is just as healthful.

There are also some flavorless olive oils, but they tend to be priced on the higher end and are not worth it. Save your money to spend on the extra-virgin oil.

Flavored oils are a recent addition on the market, and I absolutely adore them. My favorite producer of flavored oils is Zabar's, and they will ship the oils to you. Although they don't always have them all in stock, I have at one time or another bought all of the following: basil oil, fresh garlic oil, roasted garlic oil, tarragon oil (which is wonderful), oregano oil (ditto), and rosemary oil. I also recently experimented with a porcini mushroom oil, but I am not enthusiastic. These oils are best used uncooked, so save them for drizzling and for salad dressings.

Vinegars: I use a lot of balsamic vinegar because it is a simple way to both perk up existing flavors and add a caramellike nuance. There are some very different grades of balsamic vinegars. Specialty shops sell tiny cruets at astronomical prices—vinegars that have been aged and tended like family jewels. These are undeniably the very best balsamic vinegars, and if you have the resources, I suggest investing in them. Despite their diminutive size, the flasks will last for years because you are seldom asked to use more than a tablespoon or two at a time. If you see a recipe that uses in excess of a quarter cup, it is meant for a less expensive brand.

There are some very acceptable balsamic vinegars available in supermarkets that do not cost a month's rent. They are the ones I use on a normal basis.

Herbs and Spices: These two ingredients can make or break many a dish. It is imperative to use the very best, freshest herbs and the most intensely flavored spices you can find.

Most green leafy fresh herbs are pretty much interchangeable. The dish will have a different flavor, but if you choose an herb whose flavor you enjoy, this will not be a problem. If you see an herb used that you do not appreciate (as is frequently the case with cilantro, whose strong flavor offends some people), substitute one you do like. I am not a tremendous tarragon fan, and I frequently use thyme or rosemary instead. If you are fortunate enough to have a garden, or at least a sunny window, you can easily grow almost any herb, which is particularly beneficial in the winter, when fresh herbs are expensive and sparse.

Dried herbs can be replaced by fresh herbs. Use three times the amount of fresh herbs for the dried. In most cases, fresh herbs really make the difference between a good dish and a great one, so go out of your way to seek them out. This is especially true for instant gourmet cooking, because you are not using many ingredients or elaborate techniques. I know that it feels wasteful to go out and spend a dollar and a half on a bunch of fresh herbs when you only need three tablespoons and you know that the rest will wilt in your refrigerator. However, the fresh herb is worth the price because, after all, this is instant cooking, not penniless cooking. So indulge your dishes.

There is a best way to store fresh herbs, and some will last much longer than you might think. Mint, in particular, is almost indestructible. Not only is it a hearty grower but I have one handful that has lasted quite well for three weeks! I keep it in a tightly sealed container in the refrigerator with a few drops of water sprinkled over it. Most herbs will last for at least a few days if you keep them cold and moist. I store parsley and basil upright in a glass of water in the refrigerator, as if they were bouquets of flowers. This keeps them for almost a week.

Spices add depth and character to a recipe, especially when they are fresh and full of flavor. Undeniably, the most frequently used and important spices are salt and pepper. Use freshly ground sea salt for the best flavor, and always, always use freshly ground peppercorns. I also frequently use a five-pepper mix consisting of black pepper, white pepper, coriander, pink peppercorns, and allspice. It adds a special character wherever you use it; I especially like it in vinaigrettes. This alone will make a tremendous difference in your cooking.

Most spices have a shelf life of six months to two years when kept under optimal conditions (well sealed in a cool, dry, dark place). After that they will have lost most of their flavor and should be thrown out. I cannot emphasize this enough, but here's trying: if you cannot smell your spices, *throw them out,* even if you just bought them. After all, you don't know how long they were sitting in the store. Indifferent spices will lead to indifferent cooking. Furthermore, as with the herbs, since you are depending upon only a few ingredients and simple cooking techniques for flavor, the ingredients must be flavorful. Old spices are as tasty as talcum powder but not as useful.

Buy spices in bulk at health food or ethnic stores if you can; they will probably be fresher, and undoubtedly will be cheaper than the supermarket kind. I like to store them in small empty tins or glass jars, although they will be fine double-bagged in zippered sandwich bags. Don't forget to label them, or you won't be able to tell the mace from the curry powder if you happen to have a stuffy nose.

Dried Fruit and Nuts: If you have a place where you can buy your nuts in bulk, do so and you will save a good deal of money. If you buy an amount greater than what you are likely to use in the next six months, store the nuts in the freezer, tightly wrapped. The same rule applies to dried fruit.

Toasting the nuts before you use them greatly improves their flavor, making them more aromatic and intense. Of course, taking the time to toast nuts is not very speedy, but in many cases you can buy toasted nuts, especially cashews, almonds, and walnuts.

However, if you have the time, here is how to toast nuts: Spread them in a single layer on a baking sheet and bake them, stirring occasionally so they all brown evenly, for fifteen to twenty minutes in a 375° oven. The nuts should be golden brown and your kitchen filled with their sweet scent. For slivered almonds or chopped nuts, the toasting time should be shorter because the smaller pieces will brown faster. Watch them carefully.

Sometimes you will notice that your dried fruit has become too dry and hard to use. To remedy this, you can either soak the fruit in cold water or other liquid (orange juice is nice, and so is rum) for an hour or until they are soft, or you can put them in a sieve and pour the boiling liquid over them. The latter choice is quicker.

Citrus Juice and Zest: When a recipe calls for citrus zest, it signifies the colored part of the peel without the bitter white part (called the pith) underneath. To zest a citrus fruit (zest is both a noun and verb), you can use a specially made zester, which will scrape away the zest without catching any of the pith. A vegetable peeler will work just as well. After you have zested your fruit, you will probably need to grate or grind it. Chopping it finely with a sharp knife works well, as does giving it a spin in the food processor. You can also grate the zest directly off the fruit with a hand-held grater; however, I invariably end up with grated knuckles as well. It is always easier to zest fruit before you cut it. I learned this the hard way.

After you have obtained your grated zest, if you are using a recipe that also calls for the juice of the fruit, squeeze it over the zest. This will help keep the zest moist and flavorful. Citrus zests and juice also freeze well, so if you are in the mood, make a whole batch for later. This will save you future time, unless you forget to label it and it sits in the back of your freezer for a decade.

Beef and Chicken Broth: Of course, homemade broth or stock is best, but it takes time to prepare. If you live near a take-out roast chicken place, as I used to, buy the containers of stock that they invariably sell. Chinese restaurants that specialize in soups are also good places for stock. Another choice is to buy the glace de viande that is now available frozen. Just mix it up with some water and use it in place of beef broth. It packs a tremendous flavor. However, barring a convenient take-out shop or well-stocked freezer section in the supermarket, the canned variety of broth will do just fine in any of the recipes in this book. Try not to use bouillon cubes; on the whole they are high in salt and low in flavor. Many also contain monosodium glutamate, which, while you may tolerate it without a problem, your guests may not. A flavorful vegetable stock may be substituted in any recipe calling for meat stock.

Pizza Dough: Prepared pizza dough is sold either frozen in balls, or refrigerated in those peel-away cans. I definitely prefer the frozen kind, since it is usually half the price of the refrigerated kind, and tends to have a chewier, more authentic texture. The refrigerated kind is too reminiscent of bread dough for my taste. If you cannot find either type of pizza dough, you have three options left. You could either locate a sympathetic pizzeria, you could use prepared frozen or refrigerated bread dough instead, or you could make your own.

Pie Dough: Frozen and refrigerated prepared pie crusts are a wonderful product for the harried baker. Although they are not usually made with butter, and so have a less fine flavor than a homemade crust, their texture is usually quite wonderfully flaky and crisp. Prepared pie dough is easily available either frozen in a foil pie dish, or refrigerated and rolled out into a twelve-inch circle. I prefer the latter, since I can then, with a minimum of trouble, spread it into my own pie dish and flute the edges myself (which gives that homemade appearance and feel).

Eggs: All recipes in this book were tested with grade-A large eggs. Using medium or extra-large will not ruin a recipe, but it may affect the overall texture and flavor, especially if many eggs are called for.

Make sure the eggs you are using are fresh. To tell if an egg is fresh, carefully drop it into a pan of cold water. It should sink directly to the bottom, without bobbing around on top. If it floats, throw it out. This is because egg shells are porous, and the longer they sit around, the more air they absorb. The additional air makes the egg more buoyant. Eggs kept in the carton will stay fresh longer than eggs placed in the oval egg indentations in your refrigerator because their shells are better protected. If you are ever in any doubt as to the freshness of your eggs, discard them immediately.

Dairy Products: The most prevalent dairy product in this book has to be cheese, but I wrote about that in a separate section. The next most common one is butter, and that's in a separate section as well. Here, I will tell you about milk, heavy cream, sour cream, and crème fraîche.

Many of the recipes call for heavy cream. There is no acceptable substitute for real cream, so if your diet does not allow it, better to leave it out than to substitute. In baked goods, you can substitute milk for cream, but the texture may not be quite as moist. In sautés, where cream is used as a thickener for sauces, you can just eliminate it and accept the fact that your sauce will run all over your plate. I actually do that often when cooking for just myself. Remember that ultra-pasteurized cream is not as good for reducing in sauces as regular cream, so try to avoid it if you have a choice.

When milk is called for, the recipe has been tested using whole milk, although in almost every case you may substitute skim or low-fat.

Crème fraîche and sour cream, although somewhat similar in texture and flavor, are not interchangeable because sour cream will curdle when heated to boiling, and crème fraîche will not. Please use the one called for in the recipe.

Butter: Use only unsalted butter when it is specifically called for. This will be the case for most of the baked goods in this book, especially those whose flavor depends heavily upon that of butter. It is a good idea to use unsalted butter all the time because it is generally of a better quality than salted. However, if you need to clean up the last of the salted butter in your refrigerator, use it for strong-flavored foods like soups. Just be aware that the salt will cause the butter to burn faster than the unsalted kind. Mixing butter with a bit of oil will help raise the burning point of butter.

If you are worried about your cholesterol, try to use olive oil most of the time. Save the butter for special occasions.

Jams and Preserves: I use these frequently in the dessert section of this book because a high-quality fruit preserve will add incredible flavor to many sweets. Remember, you are spending too little time making your confections to skimp on the ingredients. Some of the desserts, such as mousses and fools, have only two ingredients, and if one of them is mediocre and the other is heavy cream, there not much hope for the outcome.

There are many good jams and preserves on the market, but I have not been able to test them all. However, I can unequivocally recommend American Spoon Foods as one of the best available. They have really captured the freshness of fruit in all their products. Spoon fruits without sugar are especially wonderful eaten, as the name suggests, straight from the jar with a spoon. However, in front of company, there are many simple yet elegant ways to harness all that good flavor.

Another excellent brand is Wilkin and Sons (Tiptree). Imported from England, these jams and fruit spreads have intense flavors and unusual ingredients such as kiwi fruit, guava, and passion fruit. Their lemon curd is one of the best nationally distributed brands I've tasted, although I talk more about that in the lemon curd section. (I like lemon curd so much I had to give it its own section.) The fruit spreads have less sugar and more flavor than most jams on the market. Furthermore, Wilkin and Sons are the makers of the ginger marmalade I use so often in this book. However, if you cannot find the ginger marmalade, and cannot order it from a sympathetic grocer, you can substitute orange marmalade.

Dundee, by the way, also makes a ginger marmalade that is excellent, but it is even harder to procure than Wilkin and Sons.

Lemon Curd: This product was an incredible coup for the ice cream section of this book. It gave the texture and flavor of a custard without the bother of making it. Lemon curd is also a remarkably easy tart filling. Spread it on the bottom of a baked tart shell or mound it on shortbread cookies and top with some berries and you are indulging your guests spectacularly. It is also good warmed slightly and drizzled over cut-up strawberries and nectarines.

If you cannot find Wilkin and Sons lemon curd, the most available brand, you must seek out a good less-known brand. To choose a lemon curd, look for one with the following ingredients list: sugar, lemons, butter, eggs, and maybe salt and lemon oil. If you see such things as corn syrup, fructose, lemon extract, and margarine, stay away. It won't be worth the calories.

Chocolate: Chocolate is one of the more delicious yet temperamental ingredients with which you will be working. Most of the recipes in this book call for bittersweet chocolate because that is my personal favorite. Cooking with it also gives me an excuse to keep it around the house, where I can nibble on it in the middle of the night. The quality of chocolates varies greatly, and I find that imported European chocolate is consistently better than the American brands, although there are some exceptions, such as Ghirardelli and Nestlé's Chocolat Côte d'Or. My favorite of all chocolates is Valrhona Extra Bitter, with Lindt Excellence and Caillebaut as close seconds. These chocolates are all available by mail from La Cuisine and Dean & DeLuca (see Sources, page vi). Lindt has the added attraction of being available in many supermarkets across the country.

Sometimes, when I just cannot bother with chopped chocolate and don't feel like washing out the food processor, I use semisweet chocolate chips instead. Although the flavor is perhaps not quite as fine as designer chocolates, it will still produce a fine result.

Store chocolate wrapped airtight in a cool, dry place (not the refrigerator). It will keep almost indefinitely, if you have more willpower than I. White chocolate and milk chocolate have a shorter life span than dark chocolate, and will probably last no more than a year. If your chocolate develops gray streaks, known as "bloom," it will not affect the flavor, only the appearance, which is not a factor if you are cooking with it.

equipment

In order to save both time and work, the Instant Gourmet depends on certain kitchen tools and appliances. Below is a survey of the equipment I most often use to help me cut time in the kitchen.

Food Processor and Blender: These inventions are probably the most time-saving of all the appliances mentioned in this book. I wouldn't trade my food processor for anything, even if it meant giving up my garlic press. For many recipes in this book, I direct you to use the blender and food processor interchangeably. This is true where I mention it, but is not true for everything. Both the food processor and blender are good for making dips, spreads, and purees. The blender, however, usually gives a smoother, thicker result. A food processor is better when you want your dip or spread to be slightly chunky. The food processor is also better if you need the ingredients finely chopped, as with olives for olivada. If I had to choose— which of course I don't—I would choose my food processor, since it also makes pie and cookie dough, cake batter, and pâtés; grinds nuts; whips egg whites; and grates cheese, among many other tasks. If you don't have a food processor, I advise you to buy one, even a small one. Otherwise, use your blender and a good, sharp knife.

Immersion Blender: This little gadget has completely revolutionized the way I make soup. Before, I would rarely make pureed soups because I could never puree them without making a mess. I hate working in batches because it takes so much time, and so I usually end up trying to fill the food processor as high as I can, which invariably allows the broth to leak out where the blade connects to the machine. This causes a minor flood on my counter. Occasionally I would employ both the blender and the food processor to puree the soup, and while that saved time in reducing the number of batches to puree, it took twice as long to clean the machines.

With an immersion blender I seem to puree all the soups I make. It is terrific for most vegetable and bean soups but has proved disastrous for chicken noodle soup and clam chowder. However, if you use discretion, you will probably adore this device. It is the machine I used to test the soup recipes in this book.

Microwave: I am embarrassed to admit that I do not use my microwave at all close to its potential, and so this book reflects my unenlightened state. However, if you have read all your manuals and own a copy of Barbara Kafka's incomparable *Microwave Gourmet,* you will undoubtedly be able to save even more time. Right now I use it to defrost foods, melt chocolate or butter, and cook vegetables, especially asparagus and eggplant. Feel free to use it anytime you want to in this book.

Garlic Press: This nifty device is my favorite house gift for unenlightened friends. It also makes a great wedding shower gift and is the right price for an office-party grab bag.

I use the garlic press wherever I say "minced" in a recipe—what I really mean is "pressed." Just make sure not to lose that funny little spiked piece that extrudes the leftover garlic from the holes, otherwise they are a pain to clean (a fork works in a pinch).

Salad Spinner: If you are lucky, you are going to be able to buy all your greens from the local supermarket or greengrocer, who has an abundant, fresh salad bar overflowing with washed and dried exotic greens. Back on earth, however, you will need this excellent appliance. Wash your greens in running cold water, then shake the excess water off them in the sink. Spin the greens, emptying the bowl as necessary, until they are relatively dry. Then wrap them in paper towels and place them in a plastic bag in the refrigerator. They will last for two to six days, depending on the green.

If you have one of those salad spinners that has an open grid on the bottom, don't forget to spin your lettuce in the sink, otherwise you will end up with a puddle on your counter. It's amazing how many times I have not checked the bottom of my host's salad spinner, and have ended up a soaking-wet house guest. Washing the salad greens, by the way, is the fastest way a house guest can endear himself or herself to the host.

hors d'oeuvres

White Bean and Rosemary Dip

Sometimes I substitute pink beans for the white beans in this tasty, herb-imbued dip. The texture is the same, the flavor is highly similar, but the color turns a dusty rose.

Preparation time: 10 minutes, plus chilling
Storage: 4 days refrigerated, 2 months frozen
Makes 2 cups

3 tablespoons olive oil

2 garlic cloves, minced

3 tablespoons dry white wine or water

2 cups cooked white (cannellini) beans or other canned beans, well rinsed

3 tablespoons chopped fresh rosemary, or 1 tablespoon dried

Salt and freshly ground pepper to taste

1. In a heavy, preferably nonstick, skillet, heat 1 tablespoon of the olive oil until hot but not smoking. Add the garlic and sauté for 1 minute until the garlic releases its scent and turns opaque. Stir in the wine and simmer the mixture for 30 seconds over medium heat.

2. Add the beans and cook until they absorb the liquid, about 1 minute. If the beans seem too dry, add a bit more water. Stir in the rosemary, remaining olive oil, and seasonings, and remove from heat.

3. Let the mixture cool to room temperature, and either serve immediately or store, covered, in the refrigerator for up to 5 days. If you want to use these beans for a dip, do not mash them until close to serving time. Add a bit of olive oil, if necessary, to smooth the texture. It is nice, although not imperative, to leave the puree a bit chunky.

Variation: For an earthier flavor, use brewed coffee instead of white wine.

Pesto-Stuffed Plum Tomato Halves

Stuffed plum tomato halves is an extremely attractive, easy-to-make hors d'oeuvre. Sometime I like to make a tray of these noshes and stuff them with different fillings, such as olivada (green and black), sun-dried tomato dip, blue cheese, or an herbed goat cheese.

You can also broil the tomatoes briefly and serve them as a side dish with simple grilled meats or fish.

Preparation time: 5 minutes
Storage: 1 hour, at room temperature
Serves 6–8

6 ripe plum tomatoes, sliced in half and seeded	**¼ cup pesto, prepared or homemade (page 234)**

Drizzle the insides of the tomato halves with the pesto. Serve immediately.

Variation: Substitute olivada (page 233) or Sun-Dried Tomato Dip (page 36) for the pesto. For a more substantial bite, press chopped cooked shrimp, scallops, or crab meat into the cavities of the tomatoes before drizzling with the pesto. You can also press pungent blue cheese into the tomato halves.

Sardine and Anchovy Spread with Capers

This recipe is based on one I found in one of Marcella Hazan's excellent cookbooks.

Preparation time: 10 minutes
Storage: 3 days refrigerated
Makes 1½ cups

1 can (about 4¼ ounces) best-quality skinless, boneless sardines

1 can (about 2 ounces) anchovy fillets

1 tablespoon drained capers

½ cup (1 stick) butter, at room temperature

2 teaspoons fresh thyme leaves

1. Place all the ingredients in a food processor fitted with a steel blade, or a blender.

2. Process until smooth.

Easy Empanadas

Empanadas are so easy to make with the Goya frozen empanada wrappers now available in many larger supermarkets, especially those in Hispanic neighborhoods. If you have a large freezer, buy several packages at a time when you see them. However, if you cannot find them at all, substitute wonton skins.

I like to use a chunky-style salsa for this dish—one packed with fresh tomatoes, peppers, and onions—but use whatever salsa you like best.

Preparation time: 20 minutes, plus baking

Storage: Meat mixture can be made 2 days in advance and refrigerated. Empanadas may be filled and refrigerated up to 6 hours before baking.

Serves 8–10

½ pound ground beef or turkey

½ cup salsa, prepared or homemade (page 240)

Salt and freshly ground pepper to taste

10 (1 package) frozen empanada wrappers, thawed

1 egg

1. Preheat the oven to 425° F. Line a baking sheet with foil and grease the foil.

2. In a large skillet, sauté the meat over medium-high heat, stirring and breaking up the chunks, until it is cooked, about 10 minutes. Turn off the heat and stir in the salsa, salt, and pepper.

3. Lay one of the empanada wrappers on the work surface. Spread 1 heaping table-spoon of filling on half the empanada wrapper, leaving a $\frac{1}{4}$-inch border. Fold the unfilled half of the wrapper over the filling, then decoratively pinch the seams to seal. Place the empanada on the prepared baking sheet. Repeat with the remaining wrappers and filling.

4. Beat the egg with a few drops of water until it is well mixed. Brush or dab the egg wash on the empanadas. Bake for 20 to 25 minutes, or until golden brown. Serve warm or at room temperature.

Variations: Add about $\frac{1}{4}$ cup coarsely chopped pimento-stuffed green olives or corn kernels to the filling. Or add a teaspoon or two of capers.

Cheese Empanadas

These light baked pastries also make a nice lunch when served with a large green salad.

Preparation time: 15 minutes, plus baking

Storage: Best made within 30 minutes of serving; can be filled and refrigerated up to 6 hours before baking

Serves 8–10

1 cup ricotta cheese

$\frac{1}{3}$ cup chunky salsa, prepared or homemade (page 240)

2 eggs

Salt and freshly ground pepper to taste

10 (1 package) frozen empanada wrappers, thawed

1. Preheat the oven to 425° F. Line a baking sheet with foil and grease the foil.

2. In a small bowl, mix the ricotta, the salsa, one of the eggs, and the salt and pepper until well combined.

3. Lay one of the empanada wrappers on the work surface. Spread 1 heaping tablespoon of filling on half of the empanada wrapper, leaving a $\frac{1}{4}$-inch border. Fold the unfilled half of the wrapper over the filling, then decoratively pinch the seams to seal. Place the empanada on the prepared baking sheet. Repeat with the remaining wrappers and filling.

4. Beat the remaining egg with a few drops of water until it is well mixed. Brush or dab the egg wash on the empanadas. Bake for 20 to 25 minutes, or until golden brown. Serve warm or at room temperature.

Variations: Add about $\frac{1}{3}$ cup shredded mozzarella or cheddar cheese to the filling.

Greek Cheese and Herb Spread

This makes a fabulous canapé when spread on a slice of sourdough baguette and topped with chopped marinated artichoke hearts or the pan-fried artichokes on page 177. Manouri cheese is a fresh, soft sheep's milk cheese available at specialty stores. If you cannot find it, make one of the variations below instead.

Preparation time: 5 minutes
Storage: 4 days refrigerated
Makes 1 cup

¼ pound manouri cheese

3 tablespoons olive oil,
preferably herb-flavored

3 tablespoons fresh
thyme leaves

Salt and freshly ground
pepper to taste

In the bowl of a food processor fitted with a steel blade, or a blender, process all the ingredients until smooth.

Variation: For Goat Cheese and Herb Spread, use a soft, mild goat cheese instead of the manouri. For a Bulgarian Feta and Herb Spread, substitute mild Bulgarian feta. Add garlic, either chopped raw (1 to 2 cloves) or roasted (up to 1 head; see page 231), for a nice bite.

Salmon Rillettes

This elegant spread has much more kick than a simple salmon mousse. Serve it on black bread, with a watercress garnish.

Preparation time: 10 minutes, plus chilling
Storage: 3 days refrigerated
Makes 2 cups

1 can (12 ounces) salmon

6 tablespoons (¾ stick)
butter, softened

6 tablespoons
extra-virgin olive oil

2 tablespoons Cognac

2 tablespoons minced onion

1 tablespoon
Worcestershire sauce

1. Process all the ingredients in the bowl of a food processor fitted with a steel blade or a blender until smooth.

2. Scoop the rillettes into a decorative crock and chill for at least 4 hours before serving.

Butter Bean Hummus

Using frozen butter beans (also known as lima beans) instead of chickpeas gives the traditional hummus a new twist and a pale green hue.

Preparation time: 5 minutes
Storage: 4 days refrigerated
Makes about 2 cups

1 package (10 ounces) frozen baby butter beans, thawed

¼ cup extra-virgin olive oil

2 garlic cloves, minced

¼ teaspoon powdered cumin (optional)

Salt and freshly ground pepper to taste

In a food processor fitted with a steel blade or a blender, process all the ingredients until smooth.

Grilled Portobello Mushrooms with Mozzarella

This is a modern, very elegant yet simple version of that old favorite, stuffed mushrooms. It is perfect for a large party because it tastes just as good at room temperature as it does piping hot. If you prefer to grill the mushrooms rather than broil them, please do so.

Try to find several smaller portobello mushrooms approximately the same size. If only very large ones are available, cut them in wedges just before serving.

Preparation time: 10 minutes
Storage: 2 to 3 hours at room temperature
Serves 8

1 pound portobello mushroom caps, wiped with a damp cloth	½ pound fresh mozzarella cheese, thinly sliced
3 tablespoons extra-virgin olive oil	Salt and freshly ground pepper to taste

1. Preheat the broiler or grill. Brush the mushrooms with the olive oil and top with the cheese.

2. Broil or grill the mushrooms for 3 to 5 minutes, or until the cheese is melted and slightly browned. Season to taste before serving.

Variations: Fresh or dried herbs, such as herbes de Provence, rosemary, or thyme, are always a delicious addition; just sprinkle them over the cheese after broiling. For a fuller flavor, use smoked mozzarella in place of the fresh.

Instant Tapenade

Making tapenade is not difficult, although it is time-consuming to pit all those olives. In this version, I use black olivada, which is pureed with anchovies, garlic, and herbs for a simply delicious treat. You can serve tapenade on thick slices of toast, on boiled halved red potatoes, stuffed in endive leaves or plum or cherry tomatoes, or even stuffed in celery.

Preparation time: 5 minutes
Storage: 1 week or longer refrigerated
Makes 1½ cups

1 cup olivada, prepared
or homemade (page 233)

1 tablespoon drained capers

3 anchovy fillets

2 garlic cloves

Juice of ½ lemon

⅓ cup mixed fresh
herbs such as basil, parsley, chervil

3 tablespoons olive oil

Freshly ground
pepper to taste

In a food processor fitted with a steel blade or a blender, process all the ingredients until smooth.

Variations: Substitute 2 tablespoons Cognac for the lemon juice.

Polenta Crostada with Olivada and Mozzarella

I love these small, crisp golden rectangles with their melting interiors and savory toppings. Although they are a bit messy to handle, your guests will love them. Just have plenty of napkins on hand.

Preparation time: 20 minutes
Storage: Best prepared just before serving
Serves 12–15

½ loaf polenta, prepared or homemade (page 242), cut into ½-inch slices

½ cup olivada, prepared or homemade (page 233)

¾ pound fresh mozzarella cheese, thinly sliced

1. Preheat the broiler. Spread each slice of polenta with a bit of the olivada. Top with slices of the cheese.

2. Cut the topped polenta slices lengthwise into thirds. Place them on a foil-lined baking sheet and broil for 2 to 3 minutes, until the cheese is melted. Serve immediately.

Variations: For Polenta Crostada with Salami, omit the olivada and replace the mozzarella with spicy salami or pepperoni.

Prosciutto Rolled with White or Butter Bean Dip

You can fill this simple, attractive hors d'oeuvre with almost any of the dips in this chapter. I particularly like the combination of smooth, garlicky beans with the salty meat, but the sun-dried tomato version is extremely popular as well. Experiment and you will soon find your own favorite.

Preparation time: 10–20 minutes
Storage: Several hours refrigerated
Serves 10–12

1½ cups White Bean
and Rosemary Dip (page 17) or
Butter Bean Hummus (page 24)

¼ pound prosciutto, sliced

1. To make rollups, spread a thick layer of the bean dip over one side of a slice of prosciutto. Roll up the prosciutto with the dip in the center.

2. Repeat until the dip and prosciutto are finished. Serve immediately or, if refrigerating, bring to room temperature before serving.

Variations: For Prosciutto Rollups with Sun-Dried Tomatoes, substitute the Sun-Dried Tomato Dip on page 36 for the bean dip. For Prosciutto Rollups with Greek Cheese Spread, use the Greek Cheese and Herb spread on page 22. For Prosciutto with Fava Beans, use the Fiery, Garlicky Fava Bean and Tomato Dip on page 35.

Soft Cheese with Olive Oil and Herbs

This amazingly delightful preparation can be used on whatever semisoft cheese you wish to serve. If you have some of those wonderful new herb-infused olive oils, use them here.

Tomatoes, roasted red peppers, and olives can all be added to this dish for both color and flavor, although I prefer to serve these embellishments on the side so as not to detract from the inherent simplicity of the cheese.

Preparation time: 5 minutes
Storage: Best made directly before serving
Serves 8

½ pound cheese,
cut into ¼-inch slices

2 tablespoons
extra-virgin olive oil,
preferably herb-infused

2 tablespoons chopped
fresh herbs

Lay out the cheese on a pretty serving platter. Drizzle with the olive oil and scatter the herbs on top.

Combinations: Fresh mozzarella or ricotta salata with basil, thyme, or marjoram; Bulgarian feta cheese (which is much less salty than Greek feta) with mint, tarragon, or parsley; fresh goat cheese with chives, basil, thyme, or mint; a Saint-André or a Taleggio with chopped tender celery leaves.

Roasted Figs with Parmesan

These wonderful gems are good served either hot from the oven or at room temperature. Serve them with the Grilled Portobello Mushrooms with Mozzarella on page 25 for a lovely flavor contrast between the sweet figs and the earthy mushrooms.

Preparation time: 15 minutes
Storage: Can be prepared up to 3 hours ahead
Serves 8–10

6 large, ripe figs	6 teaspoons freshly grated Parmigiano-Reggiano cheese
2 tablespoons butter, softened	2 tablespoons Cognac

1. Preheat the oven to 400° F. Slice the stems from the figs and cut the figs in half.

2. In a small bowl, combine the butter and cheese, mashing with a fork until smooth.

3. Place the fig halves on a foil-lined baking sheet. Brush them with the Cognac. Spread about 1 teaspoon of the Parmesan butter on each fig. Bake until the figs are soft and the cheese melted, 6 to 8 minutes. Serve hot, warm, or at room temperature.

Anchovy and Fennel Spread

This intense spread is wonderful to use either as a dip or as a spread on crusty whole-wheat baguettes.

Preparation time: 15 minutes

Storage: 3 days refrigerated

Makes 2 cups

1 small fennel bulb, trimmed and quartered	¼ cup extra-virgin olive oil
1 garlic clove	8 ounces cream cheese
8–12 anchovy fillets, or to taste	Salt and freshly ground pepper to taste

1. In the bowl of a food processor fitted with a steel blade, process the fennel, garlic, and anchovies until they are finely chopped.

2. Add the olive oil and cream cheese and process to a slightly chunky paste. Season with salt and pepper.

Smoked Trout Mousse

I love serving this thick, chunky mousse stuffed inside tiny boiled purple potatoes. The colors and flavors are fantastic! It is also quite good served with toasted country bread.

Preparation time: 10 minutes

Storage: 4 days refrigerated

Makes 2 cups

1 pound smoked trout fillets, boned and skinned	**¾ cup ricotta cheese**
	2 tablespoons lemon juice
2 tablespoons chopped red onion	**2 tablespoons extra-virgin olive oil**
3 tablespoons chopped fresh dill	**Salt and freshly ground pepper to taste**

In the bowl of a food processor fitted with a steel blade, process all the ingredients until smooth.

Variations: For Whitefish Mousse, substitute smoked whitefish for the trout.

Roasted Cherry Tomatoes with an Herbed Mustard Vinaigrette

Use a combination of the sweet scarlet Israeli cherry tomatoes and the tiny yellow teardrop ones for a gorgeous contrast.

Preparation time: 10 minutes
Storage: Should be assembled just before serving
Serves 8–12

1 pint cherry tomatoes, stemmed	**½ cup Herbed Vinaigrette (page 235)**
Sea salt to taste	

1. Preheat the oven to 400° F. Lay the cherry tomatoes on a baking sheet and sprinkle with the salt. Bake until they are tender, about 4 minutes.

2. Serve warm or at room temperature, drizzled with the vinaigrette.

Variations: For an even simpler version, toss the tomatoes with olive oil and salt before baking, then omit the vinaigrette.

Aquavit-Marinated Cherry Tomatoes

Use the sweetest cherry tomatoes you can find for this dish. I am particularly fond of the ones from Israel. This dish must be made at least one hour in advance.

Preparation time: 10 minutes, plus marinating
Storage: 1 day at room temperature
Serves 8–12

1 pint cherry tomatoes, stemmed	1 teaspoon caraway seeds
	Sea salt to taste
1 cup aquavit (see Note)	

1. Using the tip of a sharp knife or a toothpick, pierce each cherry tomato one or two times.

2. Mix all the ingredients in a serving bowl. Let sit at room temperature for at least 30 minutes before serving.

Note: If you don't have aquavit, substitute a flavored or plain vodka.

Spicy Peanut Dip

Dip celery, radish, and cucumber slices into this fragrant mélange.

Preparation time: 5 minutes
Storage: 3 days refrigerated
Makes 1 cup

¾ cup peanut sauce, prepared or homemade (see page 232)

¼ cup sour cream or plain yogurt

Hot red pepper flakes (optional)

In a small bowl, combine all the ingredients. Mix well.

Variations: Add 1 or 2 garlic cloves, minced.

Taramasalata

I find commercial taramasalata, a Greek fish roe puree, too fishy and strong for most of my guests, so I lighten it by adding a bit of lemon juice and yogurt. It makes a marvelous canapé when topped with dill and salmon caviar.

Preparation time: 5 minutes
Storage: 5 days refrigerated
Makes 1 cup

½ cup commercial
taramasalata

¼ cup plain yogurt or
half mayonnaise
and half yogurt

3 tablespoons lemon juice

Process all the ingredients in the bowl of a food processor or blender until smooth.

Fiery, Garlicky Fava Bean and Tomato Dip

The name says it all. Scoop it up with hot pita-bread wedges.

Preparation time: 10 minutes
Storage: 5 days refrigerated
Makes 1½ cups

1 can (12 ounces)
fava beans

Tabasco to taste

Salt to taste

2 tablespoons lemon juice

1 garlic clove, minced

½ teaspoon
ground coriander

¼ cup extra-virgin
olive oil

2 tablespoons tomato paste

Process all the ingredients in the bowl of a food processor or blender until smooth.

Sun-Dried Tomato Dip

This is my most requested dip recipe. It has an intense flavor that is positively addictive. But besides serving it as a dip or spread, I like to use it as a sauce for chicken or shrimp. Or I thin it out with some olive oil or white wine and it becomes a rich salad dressing.

Preparation time: 5 minutes
Storage: 5 days refrigerated
Makes 1½ cups

¼ cup oil-packed
sun-dried tomatoes

2 garlic cloves, minced

2 teaspoons
drained capers

2 teaspoons fresh
thyme leaves

⅔ cup mayonnaise

⅔ cup plain yogurt

Salt and freshly ground
pepper to taste

1. In a food processor fitted with a steel blade or a blender, process the sun-dried tomatoes, garlic, capers, and thyme until finely chopped.

2. Add the mayonnaise, yogurt, salt, and pepper and pulse to combine. Refrigerate until needed.

soups

Light Tomato Broth with Herbs

This fast and easy broth can be embellished in myriad ways—with vegetables, sliced cooked chicken, pasta, beans, sausage, seafood. I have included several of my favorite renditions below.

Don't be put off by the V-8, a suggestion given to me by Richard Flaste; it adds both richness and body.

If you would like a garlicky flavor, add four or five smashed cloves to the broth, which can easily be removed with a slotted spoon after simmering.

Preparation time: 10 minutes
Storage: 4 days refrigerated, 6 months frozen
Makes 1½ quarts

1 quart chicken or
vegetable broth

1 cup dry white wine

1 cup V-8 juice

Generous pinch of
herbes de Provence

Dash of Tabasco
(optional)

Salt and freshly ground
pepper to taste
(optional)

1. Mix all the ingredients in a large saucepan and bring to a boil over high heat.

2. Lower the heat and simmer the mixture for 5 minutes.

3. Remove from the heat and correct the seasonings, if necessary.

Tortellini Soup with Pesto

This recipe is actually more of a pasta dish than a soup, with fresh tortellini immersed in a light, refreshing sauce of tomato broth and pesto.

Preparation time: 20 minutes
Storage: 3 days refrigerated
Serves 4

1 pound fresh tortellini

1 recipe Light Tomato Broth with Herbs (page 37)

¼ cup pesto, prepared or homemade (page 234)

1. In a large saucepan, bring the tortellini to a boil with enough salted water to cover. Cook the tortellini until tender, about 10 minutes. Drain.

2. In a medium saucepan over high heat, bring the tomato broth to a boil. Remove from the heat.

3. To serve, divide the tortellini among 4 soup plates. Cover each with some of the tomato broth, then garnish the top of each with 1 tablespoon of the pesto. Serve immediately.

Mozzarella and Salami Soup with Olivada

This rich soup has a wonderful texture from the molten mozzarella cubes, which soften but never quite dissolve in the broth. The salami adds a nice spicy note to the soup, but it can easily be omitted if you prefer a vegetarian version.

Preparation time: 10 minutes
Storing: 3 days refrigerated
Serves 6

1 recipe Light Tomato Broth
with Herbs (page 37)

½ cup frozen or fresh peas

3 tablespoons black or green
olivada, prepared or homemade
(page 233)

¼ cup coarsely chopped
salami, preferably garlic-flavored

1 pound fresh mozzarella,
cut into 1-inch cubes

3 tablespoons chopped
fresh basil or parsley

1. In a large saucepan over high heat, bring the broth and peas to a boil.

2. Remove from the heat and stir in the remaining ingredients. Serve immediately.

Minted Sugar Snap Pea Soup with Beet Cream

This colorful soup is excellent served either with or without the accompanying beet cream. It makes a very impressive first course.

Preparation time: 15 minutes
Storing: 3 days refrigerated, 3 months frozen
Serves 4–6

2 packages (10 ounces each)
frozen sugar snap peas, or
1 pound fresh
sugar snap peas, trimmed

1 large potato, peeled
and thinly sliced

1 garlic clove, peeled

1 quart chicken or
vegetable broth

3 tablespoons heavy cream
or whole milk

Salt and freshly ground
pepper to taste (optional)

2 teaspoons balsamic vinegar

Beet Cream (recipe follows)

1. In a large saucepan, combine the sugar snap peas, potato, garlic, and broth. Bring to a boil over high heat. Lower the heat and simmer until the potato slices are tender, about 10 minutes. Puree the soup with a blender or food processor until it is very smooth.

2. Return the soup to the saucepan and add the cream. Simmer the mixture for 1 minute. Add salt and pepper and stir in the vinegar. Serve with swirls of Beet Cream, if desired.

Beet Cream

Preparation: 5 minutes
Storage: 5 days refrigerated
Makes ½ cup

¼ cup sliced cooked
beets (either canned or fresh)

¼ cup sour cream or
plain yogurt

In a food processor or blender, combine the beets and sour cream. Process or blend until the mixture is smooth and pink.

Succotash Soup with Smithfield Ham

Here is a creamy soup that is not overly rich, with a complex sweet and salty flavor from the corn and the ham. It is a wonderful main-course soup, especially for a luncheon.

If you cannot get good Smithfield ham, use a domestic prosciutto instead.

Preparation time: 10 minutes
Storage: 4 days refrigerated, 3 months frozen
Serves 4–6

2 cups chicken or vegetable broth	3 tablespoons chopped Smithfield ham
1 package (10 ounces) frozen baby lima beans	3 tablespoons chopped fresh basil or parsley
1 package (10 ounces) frozen sweet corn kernels	Salt and freshly ground pepper to taste
¼ cup heavy cream or whole milk	

1. In a large saucepan, combine the broth and lima beans over high heat and bring the mixture to a boil. Let the mixture boil for 2 minutes, then reduce the heat to medium.

2. Stir in the corn, cream, and ham and simmer the mixture for 2 minutes more. Stir in the basil, salt, and pepper.

3. If desired, puree about 1½ cups of the soup in a blender or food processor, then return the puree to the rest of the soup. This gives the soup a heartier texture.

White Bean Broth with Sage and Goat Cheese Croutons

This is a wonderful, versatile broth that can be served alone or with the Goat Cheese Croutons as an elegant first course. Or serve it as a light sauce for meats (such as veal) and seafood, such as in Tuna in White Bean Broth with Sage (page 161).

Feel free to substitute other fresh herbs for the sage, such as rosemary or thyme.

Preparation time: 10–15 minutes
Storage: 4 days refrigerated, 3 months frozen
Serves 4

1 can (19 ounces) cannellini or other white beans

2 cups chicken or vegetable broth

2 tablespoons lemon juice

Salt and freshly ground pepper to taste

3 tablespoons chopped fresh sage

Goat Cheese Croutons (optional; recipe follows)

1. In a blender or food processor, puree the beans and their liquid until they are smooth.

2. In a large saucepan, bring the broth and white bean puree to a boil over high heat. Reduce heat to low and stir in the lemon juice and salt and pepper.

3. At this point, you may either stir the sage in and serve as is, or strain the soup first. To strain, pass the broth through a sieve, and then return it to low heat. Stir in the sage and cook for 1 minute. Serve either by itself or with the croutons.

Goat Cheese Croutons

These tasty toasts are also good to serve with salads.

Preparation time: 7 minutes
Storage: 1 day before broiling
Serves 6

6 slices French or Italian bread	**2 ounces mild goat cheese, such as Montrachet**
1 tablespoon butter, softened	**Freshly ground pepper to taste**

1. Preheat the broiler. Spread the bread slices with the butter, then with an equal amount of the goat cheese. Arrange them on a broiler-safe baking sheet. Grind the fresh pepper over the croutons.

2. Broil the croutons until the cheese browns, 1 to 2 minutes. Serve immediately.

Spiced Pumpkin Soup with Caramelized Apple

For a perfect autumn first course, serve this silky, rich soup with roasted chestnuts for nibbling.

Preparation time: 5 minutes
Storage: 3 days refrigerated, 3 months frozen
Serves 4–6

1 can (16 ounces) solid-pack pumpkin puree	**Freshly grated nutmeg to taste**
2½ cups chicken or vegetable broth	**Salt and freshly ground pepper to taste**
1 tablespoon fresh thyme, or 1 teaspoon dried	**Caramelized Apple (optional; recipe follows)**
Small pinch of ground cinnamon	

1. In a large saucepan, bring all the ingredients except the apples to a boil over medium heat. Reduce heat and simmer the mixture for 2 minutes.

2. Correct seasonings and serve with the Caramelized Apple, if desired.

Caramelized Apple

This sweet-tart apple recipe has a multitude of uses: to garnish game and meats (especially pork); to enliven an endive salad; or to top ice cream or yogurt. Don't just limit it to soup.

Make sure to use a firm, tart green apple for this recipe, such as Granny Smith.

Preparation time: 10 minutes
Storage: 4 days refrigerated
Makes ½ cup

½ cup green apple peeled,
cored, and diced in ½-inch pieces

¼ cup water

2 tablespoons butter

1 tablespoon sugar

1 tablespoon balsamic vinegar

1. In a large skillet, combine the apple, water, and butter. Cook the mixture over high heat until the water evaporates and the apples are tender, 2 to 4 minutes.

2. Stir in the sugar and vinegar and cook the mixture, stirring, until the apple turns a ruddy brown and caramelizes, about 3 minutes. Serve immediately.

Black Velvet Soup

Preparation time: 10 minutes
Storage: 3 days refrigerated
Serves 4–6

3 cans (15 ounces each)
black beans

2 cups beef, chicken,
or vegetable broth

¼ cup dry sherry

½ cup sour cream,
crème fraîche, or plain yogurt

3 tablespoons chopped
fresh basil or parsley

Salt and freshly ground
pepper to taste

1. In a blender or food processor, puree the beans and their liquid until smooth.

2. In a large saucepan, bring the bean puree, broth, and sherry to a boil over medium heat. Remove the pan from the heat and stir in the sour cream and basil. Correct the seasonings and serve immediately.

Cold Cucumber Soup with Shrimp and Tarragon

This delicious soup happens to be very low in fat. Dill can replace the tarragon if you prefer, and scallops can easily replace the shrimp, although the color is not as pretty.

For an even more pronounced tarragon flavor, use tarragon-flavored olive oil. Zabar's has an excellent one (see Sources, page vi).

Preparation time: 15 minutes

Storage: Soup 3 days refrigerated; shrimp should be cooked at the last minute.

Serves 4

2 medium cucumbers, peeled, seeded, and chopped	Salt and freshly ground pepper to taste
1½ cups nonfat plain yogurt	12 large shrimp, cleaned
1 garlic clove, coarsely chopped, or 1 teaspoon prepared minced garlic	1 tablespoon extra-virgin olive oil
2 tablespoons chopped fresh tarragon	

1. In a food processor or blender, puree the cucumbers, yogurt, garlic, tarragon, and seasonings. Chill the mixture in the refrigerator until serving time.

2. When ready to serve, place the shrimp in a steamer basket and steam until they just turn pink, about 2 minutes. Alternatively, you may cook the shrimp in the microwave, covered in microwavable plastic wrap, for 1 to 2 minutes, checking every 30 seconds.

3. To serve, divide the soup among 4 soup plates and drizzle with the olive oil. Top each plate with 3 hot shrimp. Serve immediately.

salads

Perfect Green Salad

Of course, the most time-consuming and dreary task in making a green salad is washing and drying those greens. Luckily, it is now easy to find all kinds of washed greens packaged at the supermarket or available in salad bars. Mesclun—a mixture of baby greens—is usually sold washed and table-ready, as is fresh spinach, which is also good for a salad. However, if you cannot find table-ready greens, wash the greens in plenty of running cold water and dry them in a salad spinner.

Serves time: 5 minutes
Storage: None
Serves 6

8 cups mixed greens, washed and dried	**½ cup vinaigrette of choice**

In a large salad bowl, toss the greens with the vinaigrette. Serve immediately.

Variation: Add up to 1 cup of chopped mixed fresh herbs, such as parsley, chervil, basil, tarragon, thyme, chives, and oregano.

Mesclun Salad with Baked Nutted Goat Cheese

Use the table-ready mesclun available in most supermarkets to make this luscious salad.

Preparation time: 10 minutes
Storage: None
Serves 4

½ cup finely chopped toasted hazelnuts

1 small log goat cheese, sliced into 4 rounds

6 cups mesclun or mixed greens, washed

½ cup hazelnut vinaigrette (page 238)

1. Preheat the oven to 400° F.

2. Place the nuts in a small bowl. Add the goat cheese and toss to coat the disks with the nuts. Place the nut-covered disks on a baking sheet and bake until they are soft, about 5 minutes.

3. In a large bowl, toss the mesclun with the vinaigrette. Divide the salad among 4 plates. Top with the warm goat cheese. Serve immediately.

Cumin Broccoli Salad

No, you don't have to cook the broccoli; the marinade softens and "cooks" it much in the way ceviche is cooked.

Preparation time: 15 minutes, plus chilling
Storage: 3 days refrigerated
Serves 6–8

2 heads broccoli,
trimmed into florets

½ cup extra-virgin olive oil

1 teaspoon cumin seeds

Pinch of hot red
pepper flakes

2 garlic cloves, minced

2 tablespoons
red wine vinegar

Salt to taste

1. Place the broccoli florets in a large bowl.

2. In a skillet over medium heat, heat the olive oil until it is hot but not smoking. Add the cumin seeds and toast them, stirring, for 15 seconds. Turn off the heat.

3. In a small bowl, combine the cumin oil, red pepper flakes, garlic, vinegar, and salt. Mix well. Pour this mixture over the broccoli, tossing to coat.

4. Marinate the broccoli for at least 2 hours in the refrigerator.

Arugula, Orange, and Red Onion Salad

Preparation time: 10 minutes
Storage: None
Serves 6

> **3 cups arugula
> (2 small bunches),
> washed and dried**
>
> **3 navel oranges,
> peeled and cubed**

> **1 small red onion,
> thinly sliced**
>
> **½ cup Basic or Walnut
> Vinaigrette (pages 235, 238)**

In a large bowl, mix the arugula, oranges, and onion with the dressing, tossing to coat. Serve immediately.

Variations: For a Watercress, Walnut, and Orange Salad, substitute watercress for the arugula, eliminate the red onion, and add ¾ cup toasted walnuts. Dress with Walnut Vinaigrette.

Watercress, Avocado, and Salsa Salad

Make sure to buy the nubby black-skinned Hass avocados from California. They have the most buttery flesh.

Preparation time: 5 minutes
Storage: None
Serves 6

4 cups (2 bunches)
watercress leaves,
washed and dried

½ cup Fresh and
Chunky Salsa (page 240)

½ ripe Hass avocado,
peeled, pitted, and cubed

Place the watercress on a large platter. Top with the avocado and salsa. Serve immediately.

Tomato Salad with Basil

This simple salad depends on fully ripened tomatoes and fresh basil for its flavor.

Preparation time: 5 minutes
Storage: 2 hours at room temperature
Serves 8

8 large, ripe tomatoes,
sliced

⅓ cup extra-virgin
olive oil

Salt and freshly ground
pepper to taste

1 garlic clove, minced

½ cup fresh basil
leaves, chopped

1. Lay the tomatoes out on a platter. Drizzle the olive oil over the tomatoes, sprinkle them with the salt and pepper, and top with the garlic and basil. Serve immediately, or let the salad marinate at room temperature for up to 2 hours.

Variation: Add sliced goat cheese, mozzarella, or brie to this salad to make it more substantial. Also, sprinkle on some black or green olives and/or chopped red onion.

Celery and Blue Cheese Salad

This crunchy salad combines cool chopped celery with pungent soft blue cheese. It's a wonderful juxtaposition.

Preparation time: 5 minutes
Storage: 1 day refrigerated
Serves 6

3 cups sliced celery

⅓ cup Basic or
Balsamic Vinaigrette
(page 235)

⅔ cup crumbled
blue cheese

In a large bowl, combine the celery, vinaigrette, and blue cheese. Toss well.

Variations: For a different type of crunch, add up to 1 cup toasted walnuts. The earthiness of the nuts really complements the celery.

Cucumber Salad

This fat-free salad will last for up to a week in the refrigerator, making it a good thing to keep on hand for lazy summer days when you know you should eat a salad but it seems too intimidating to make anything at all.

Preparation time: 5 minutes, plus chilling
Storage: 1 week refrigerated
Serves 4

**1 European cucumber,
very thinly sliced**

**½ cup white
wine vinegar**

½ cup water

1 tablespoon sugar

**2 tablespoons chopped
fresh dill**

**Salt and freshly ground
pepper to taste**

1. In a large bowl, combine all the ingredients, tossing well.

2. Refrigerate the salad for at least 1 hour before serving.

Fennel Salad with Walnuts and Oranges

This lovely salad is perfect in the winter, when fennel and oranges are at their best.

Preparation time: 5 minutes
Storage: 1 day refrigerated
Serves 4–6

**2 fennel bulbs,
trimmed and sliced**

**2 navel oranges,
peeled and sliced crosswise**

⅓ cup toasted walnuts

2 tablespoons olive oil

**Salt and freshly ground
pepper to taste**

1. Lay the fennel slices out on a serving platter. Top with the orange slices and walnuts.

2. Drizzle with the olive oil and sprinkle the salt and pepper over the salad.

Variations: For Fennel Salad with Parmesan and Walnuts, omit the oranges and add freshly shaved or grated Parmesan cheese (about 1 ounce, or ¼ cup).

Greek Salad

With all the different vegetables in this salad it is best, as always, to get as many of them as you can pre-cut from a salad bar. Otherwise it ends up being a lot of work.

Preparation time: 15 minutes
Storage: None
Serves 4–6

6 cups romaine lettuce
(about 1 head),
washed and dried

1 cup diced tomato

1 cup diced green bell pepper

1 cup diced cucumber

½ cup diced red onion

½ cup sliced celery

¼ pound feta
cheese, crumbled

¼ cup kalamata olives

½ cup Garlic
Vinaigrette (page 238)

2 tablespoons
chopped fresh oregano

In a large bowl, combine all the ingredients and toss to combine them. Serve immediately.

Warm Potatoes Vinaigrette

This lovely salad has entirely replaced the standard potato salad in my repertoire. If you can get only the larger red potatoes, quarter them.

Preparation time: 20 minutes

Storage: 2 days refrigerated

Serves 4

1½ pounds very small red potatoes, scrubbed and halved	**1 teaspoon Worcestershire sauce**
¾ cup Mustard Vinaigrette (page 235)	**3 tablespoons chopped fresh parsley**

1. Bring a large pot of salted water to a boil. Add the potatoes and cook until they are easily pierced with a fork, 10 to 15 minutes.

2. Drain the potatoes and place them in a large serving bowl. Toss with the vinaigrette, Worcestershire sauce, and parsley. Serve immediately, or let cool to room temperature.

Variation: Add up to ½ cup sour cream to the salad for a creamy texture.

Middle Eastern Carrot Salad

This perfumed salad is utterly delicious. I usually make the variation with golden raisins, but it is good either way. For a fat-free salad, simply eliminate the olive oil.

Preparation time: 5 minutes

Storage: 2 days refrigerated

Serves 4–6

1 pound carrots, shredded (about 2½ cups)	**Few drops of orange flower water**
3 tablespoons orange juice	**Salt and freshly ground pepper to taste**
2 tablespoons extra-virgin olive oil	
1 tablespoon lemon juice	

Combine all the ingredients in a large bowl, tossing well.

Variations: Add up to 1 cup golden raisins and a dash of freshly grated nutmeg. Or skip the olive oil and use 2 tablespoons good prepared or homemade mayonnaise.

Mushroom and Provolone Salad

Sliced mushrooms are another good salad bar staple. If you don't have aged provolone on hand, substitute a nice Parmesan instead.

Preparation time: 5 minutes
Storage: 1 day refrigerated
Serves 4–6

½ pound (3 cups) white mushrooms, cleaned and sliced	**⅓ cup chopped cilantro**
	⅓ cup Lemon Vinaigrette (page 236)
2 ounces aged provolone, shaved or grated	

Toss all the ingredients together in a large bowl.

Zucchini Salad with Curry

I love to serve this unusual salad in the winter.

Make sure to use small zucchini, or a combination of zucchini and summer squash, if available.

Preparation time: 10 minutes
Storage: 4 hours refrigerated
Serves 6

6 small zucchini, scrubbed

1 tablespoon extra-virgin olive oil

3 tablespoons plain yogurt

½ teaspoon curry powder

Salt and freshly ground pepper to taste

1. In a food processor using the grater disk, grate the zucchini.

2. Place the grated zucchini in a large bowl and toss with the remaining ingredients. Serve immediately or within 4 hours.

Tricolored Pepper Salad

This dish also works well with the Silver Palate's Caesar salad dressing, one of the only bottled salad dressings I like. Use it in place of homemade vinaigrette.

Remember that most salad bars have sliced bell peppers of different colors, although slicing peppers is relatively quick. If you are slicing the peppers yourself, use one of each color or three in total of any color.

Preparation time: 10 minutes
Storage: 2 days refrigerated
Serves 4–6

**1 cup sliced
red bell pepper**

**1 cup sliced
green bell pepper**

**1 cup sliced
yellow bell pepper**

**½ cup Garlic or
Mustard Vinaigrette
(pages 238, 235)**

1. In a small bowl or serving dish, combine all the ingredients. Toss to combine.

2. Serve immediately, or let the salad marinate at room temperature for up to 1 hour, or up to 2 days in the refrigerator. Bring to room temperature before serving.

Hardy Greens and Tuna Salad

I love to serve this salad with the tomato variation below. It makes a perfect luncheon entree in the summertime.

Preparation time: 15 minutes
Storage: None.
Serves 2-4

1 tablespoon olive oil

Salt and freshly ground pepper to taste

1 pound tuna steaks, about 1 inch thick

6 cups torn hardy greens, such as watercress, frisée, Belgium endive, spinach, arugula

$^2/_3$ cup Mustard Vinaigrette (page 235)

1. Preheat the broiler.

2. Rub the olive oil, salt, and pepper onto the tuna steaks. Broil until the tuna is rare, 3 to 4 minutes per side, or to taste. Let the tuna rest until cool enough to handle, then slice it on the bias into thin slices.

3. Toss the greens with $^1/_2$ cup of the dressing. Place the greens on a serving platter and top with the tuna. Drizzle tuna with the remaining vinaigrette. Serve immediately.

Variations: Add 2 large ripe tomatoes, seeded and cubed, and/or 2 cups cubed boiled potatoes to the salad, but you may have to add more vinaigrette, or at least more salt and pepper.

Rice Salad

You can use all white rice or part white and part brown rice to make this colorful salad. To obtain the cooked rice, you can cook it yourself or do what I do—pick it up from a Chinese restaurant. It's best to mix this salad while the rice is still warm; it absorbs the dressing better.

Preparation time: 10 minutes
Storage: None
Serves 6–8

4 cups cooked rice
(2 pints from a take-out place)

¾ cup Basic
Vinaigrette (page 235)

6 ripe plum
tomatoes, diced

⅓ cup black olives

¼ cup diced celery

¼ cup diced red onion

Salt and freshly ground
pepper to taste

In a large bowl, combine all the ingredients, tossing to coat them with the vinaigrette. Taste and adjust the seasonings.

Tabbouleh Salad

This bright green salad is incredibly refreshing when served chilled on a hot day.

Preparation time: 15 minutes, plus soaking
Storage: 3 days refrigerated
Serves 6–8

2 cups water

1 cup bulgur wheat

1 small red onion, chopped

½ cup chopped fresh mint

½ cup chopped fresh parsley

1 teaspoon lemon zest

3 tablespoons extra-virgin olive oil

Salt and freshly ground pepper to taste

1. In a large bowl, combine the water and tabbouleh. Let sit at room temperature for 30 minutes or until the bulgur is softened.

2. Fluff the bulgur with a fork. Mix in the onion, mint, parsley, lemon zest, olive oil, and salt and pepper.

Variations: Add any or all of the following: 1 cup cubed seeded tomatoes; black olives; 1 cup cubed cucumber.

Couscous Salad with Chickpeas, Orange, and Mint

Preparation time: 15 minutes, plus soaking
Storage: 3 days refrigerated
Serves 4–6

1 cup couscous

1 cup boiling beef
or chicken broth

6 tablespoons orange juice

1 can (19 ounces)
chickpeas, drained

½ cup chopped fresh
mint, basil, or parsley

1 teaspoon vinegar
(sherry vinegar is recommended), or
2 teaspoons lemon juice

Salt and freshly ground
pepper to taste

1. In a large bowl, combine the couscous and boiling broth. Cover the bowl with a dish towel and let sit at room temperature for about 12 minutes, or until the couscous is softened.

2. Fluff the couscous with a fork. Mix in the orange juice, chickpeas, herbs, vinegar, and salt and pepper.

Variations: Add any or all of the following: 1 to 2 tablespoons extra-virgin olive oil (for flavor and gloss), 2 tablespoons finely chopped red onion or scallion, 1 minced garlic clove, 2 tablespoons chopped black olives, ½ cup chopped vegetables (cucumber, celery, carrots, red or green peppers, watercress leaves). Of course, 1 cup of chopped orange sections is a wonderful addition as well.

Pasta Salad with Cherry Tomatoes and Ricotta Salata

I had a version of this lovely salad at a gathering of the New York Women's Culinary Alliance. I never discovered who made it, but it was just perfect in its simplicity. Make sure you use a fragrant and flavorful olive oil, and if you can, half red and half yellow cherry tomatoes.

Preparation time: 15 minutes
Storage: 1 day refrigerated
Serves 4–6

1 pound penne

1 pint cherry tomatoes, halved

3 tablespoons chopped fresh basil

1 tablespoon fresh thyme leaves

1 garlic clove, minced

¼ cup extra-virgin olive oil

¾ pound ricotta salata, crumbled

Salt and freshly ground pepper to taste

1. Cook the penne according to the package directions.

2. Meanwhile, prepare the dressing: In a large serving bowl, combine the tomatoes, basil, thyme, garlic, oil, cheese, salt, and pepper. Mix well.

3. Drain the pasta and add it to the dressing. Toss to combine. Serve immediately or refrigerate until ready. Bring to room temperature before serving.

Variations: For a more substantial salad, add up to 2 cups cooked shrimp, scallops, or cubed chicken. You may need to add more olive oil and salt and pepper to balance the flavors.

Pasta Salad with Pesto and Peppers

I like to use a substantial pasta for this salad. Orecchiette—small ear-shaped pasta with a thick texture—are my preference, but you can substitute shells, bow ties, or other pasta if you wish.

Preparation time: 15 minutes
Storage: 1 day refrigerated
Serves 4–6

1 pound orecchiette

1 cup pesto, prepared or homemade (page 234)

1 cup diced roasted peppers

1. Cook the pasta according to the package directions. Drain and place in a serving bowl.

2. Add the pesto and toss well. Top with the peppers and serve immediately or refrigerate until ready. Bring to room temperature before serving.

Variations: For a lighter salad, substitute plain yogurt for $\frac{1}{2}$ cup of the pesto.

Green Bean Salad with Walnuts and Pecorino

This lovely salad can be served warm, cold, or at room temperature. Since it will not

wilt, it is a good choice to bring on a picnic or to a potluck.

Preparation time: 15 minutes
Storage: 3 days refrigerated
Serves 4–6

1½ pounds green beans

1 cup shelled walnuts

2 ounces pecorino
cheese, diced

⅓ cup Basic Vinaigrette
(page 235)

1. Bring a large pot of salted water to a boil. Add the green beans and cook about 2
minutes or until they are done to your taste. Drain them well and refresh under cold
water.

2. Place the beans in a large bowl. Add the walnuts, cheese, and vinaigrette and toss
well. Serve immediately or refrigerate until ready. Bring to room temperature before
serving.

Variation: Substitute wax beans for the green beans. Add some chopped red onion for color and flavor,
if desired.

snacks and sandwiches

Sun-Dried Tomato and Basil Lavash Rolls

These wonderful little mouthfuls are the inspiration of the very talented Samara Farber, who introduced them to the New York catering firm Flavors, where she was a chef.

They are wonderful to serve as a party canapé, because they can be made completely in advance (in fact, they are easier to cut if they are chilled first), then sliced as the guests arrive.

Lavash is a large, thin flat bread baked on hot stones. It is available in any Middle Eastern specialty shop, usually sold in bags next to the more familiar pita bread.

Preparation time: 10 minutes, plus chilling
Storage: 1 day, well wrapped in plastic and refrigerated
Makes 24 pieces

2 tablespoons oil-packed sun-dried tomatoes	1 lavash, about 16 inches in diameter
1 cup whipped cream cheese	1 cup fresh basil leaves, plus additional for garnish

1. In a food processor fitted with a steel blade, combine the tomatoes and cream cheese and process until the mixture is completely smooth.

2. Place the lavash on a work surface. Spread the cream cheese mixture over the lavash in a thin, even layer. Top with the basil leaves.

3. Cut the lavash in half. Starting with the cut side, roll up each piece tightly, jelly-roll style. Wrap the lavash rolls in plastic wrap and refrigerate for at least 15 minutes before slicing.

4. When ready to serve, use a serrated knife to trim the ends (which will be uneven). Then slice each roll into 12 pieces and arrange them on a serving platter. They are pretty when garnished with more fresh basil.

Smoked Salmon Lavash Rolls

These little morsels are an elegant and unusual way to serve smoked salmon. You may never buy bagels again.

Preparation time: 10 minutes, plus chilling
Storage: 1 day, well wrapped in plastic and refrigerated
Makes 24 pieces

1 lavash, about 16 inches in diameter

1 cup plain or scallion whipped cream cheese

2 tablespoons fresh lemon juice

4 ounces thinly sliced smoked salmon

Freshly ground pepper

1. Place the lavash on a work surface. Spread the cream cheese over the lavash in a thin, even layer. Sprinkle the lemon juice over the cream cheese and then top with the smoked salmon. Grind plenty of pepper over the salmon.

2. Cut the lavash in half. Starting with the cut side, roll up each piece tightly, jelly-roll style. Wrap the lavash rolls in plastic wrap and refrigerate for at least 15 minutes before slicing.

3. When ready to serve, use a serrated knife to trim the ends (which will be uneven). Then slice each roll into 12 pieces and arrange them on a serving platter.

Variations: Substitute other smoked fish, such as flaked smoked trout, for the salmon. To make Mozzarella and Salmon Rolls, substitute $\frac{1}{2}$ pound thinly sliced mozzarella for the cream cheese and add $\frac{1}{2}$ cup fresh basil leaves to the rolls. This is especially nice for a party, although it is a bit more difficult to cut neatly.

Pan Bagna

When I was a little girl, my parents went through a pan bagna stage while we were vacationing in southern France. Every morning my father and I would walk to the local *boulangerie* for fresh croissants, pains au chocolat, and a fat, round country bread. After we consumed our breakfast we would assemble the pan bagna. The round bread was cut in half and the insides pulled out. The crust was layered with tuna, anchovies, tomatoes, black and green olives (never pitted), chopped celery or cucumber, sweet onion, hard-boiled eggs, and a garlic-studded mustard vinaigrette. The bread was then wrapped well in plastic and foil, and my sister and I took turns sitting on the colossal sandwich until it flattened out and the bread soaked up all that vinaigrette.

Preparation time: 10 minutes, plus pressing

Storage: 2 days, well wrapped in plastic wrap and refrigerated

Serves 4

1 round country loaf, about 1 pound

2 cans (6 to 7 ounces each) oil-packed tuna

½ cup sliced sweet onion

½ cup diced cucumber or celery

1 cup diced tomato

¼ cup mixed green and black olives

8 anchovy fillets

2 hard-boiled eggs, peeled and sliced (optional)

¼ cup fresh basil leaves

½ cup Mustard Vinaigrette (page 235)

1 garlic clove, minced

Salt and freshly ground pepper to taste

1. Slice the bread in half horizontally. Pull out some but not all of the soft white crumbs and save those for another use.

2. Place the tuna in a large bowl and break it up with a fork. Add the onion, cucumber or celery, tomato, and olives and toss to combine. Place this mixture on the bottom half of the bread. Layer the anchovies, eggs, and basil over the tuna mixture.

3. In a small bowl, combine the vinaigrette and garlic. Pour two-thirds of this mixture over the tuna-stuffed bread half. Drizzle the remaining vinaigrette over the other bread half and place it over the filling.

4. Wrap the bread in several layers of plastic wrap and foil (so it won't leak) and then have your child sit on it for a while. Alternatively, place a large, heavy frying pan on top and weight it down with some heavy cans. Let it sit for at least 30 minutes before serving.

Fresh Goat Cheese Quesadillas

I usually serve these at parties as an hors d'oeuvre, but they are equally wonderful served with a small mesclun salad as a first course. Made with large twelve-inch tortillas, they are a meal.

I generally prefer wheat tortillas, but if you like corn better, by all means use those. Whole-wheat tortillas make a nice change as well.

Preparation time: 15 minutes
Storage: refrigerated, then baked
Serves 4 as first course, 8–10 as hors d'oeuvre

8 small (6- or 7-inch)
flour tortillas

6 ounces fresh goat cheese,
crumbled or cubed

1 cup chunky salsa,
prepared or homemade
(page 240)

1. Preheat the oven to 450° F. Line a baking sheet with foil.

2. Lay 4 tortillas on the baking sheet. Divide the goat cheese among them and top with the salsa. Lay the remaining tortillas on top of the salsa. (If storing, cover tightly and refrigerate.)

3. Bake the quesadillas until the cheese is melted, about 10 minutes. Cut into wedges and serve immediately.

Aged Jack, Corn, and Cilantro Quesadilla

Aged jack cheese has a harder texture and more pungent flavor than regular Monterey jack. If you cannot find it, you can substitute regular jack cheese or another hard grating cheese such as an aged cheddar or a pecorino (highly untraditional but quite delicious).

Preparation time: 15 minutes
Storage: refrigerate, then bake
Serves 4 as first course, 8–10 as hors d'oeuvre

8 small (6- or 7-inch) flour tortillas

2 cups (about ½ pound) shredded aged Monterey jack cheese

1 cup frozen or fresh corn kernels

¼ cup chopped cilantro

1. Preheat the oven to 450° F. Line a baking sheet with foil.

2. Lay 4 tortillas on the baking sheet. Divide the jack cheese between them, and top with the corn and cilantro. Lay the remaining tortillas on top of the cilantro. (If storing, cover tightly and refrigerate.)

3. Bake the quesadillas until the cheese is melted, about 10 minutes. Cut into wedges and serve immediately.

Watercress and Mozzarella Burritos

I was served a variation of this dish at a wonderful Mexican restaurant outside of San Antonio, Texas.

Preparation time: 15 minutes
Storage: None
Serves 4 as first course, 2 as light entree

2 tablespoons olive oil

4 cups (2 bunches) watercress, washed

1 garlic clove, minced

Salt and freshly ground pepper to taste

4 large (12-inch) flour tortillas

1 cup (4 ounces) sliced or shredded fresh mozzarella cheese

1. Preheat the oven to 450° F. Line a baking sheet with foil.

2. In a large skillet over medium heat, heat the olive oil until it is hot but not smoking. Add the watercress and the garlic and sauté until the watercress is wilted and the garlic opaque, 1 to 2 minutes. Stir in the salt and pepper.

3. Lay 2 of the tortillas on the baking sheet. Spread each with $\frac{1}{4}$ cup of the cheese. Divide half of the watercress mixture between them over the cheese. Roll up the tortillas loosely. Repeat with the remaining ingredients.

3. Bake the burritos until the cheese just melts, about 5 minutes. Serve immediately.

Variations: Top each burrito with a fried egg after baking. When the yolk is split, it makes a lush sauce.

Simple Tomato Bruschetta

Bruschetta is more than an open-faced sandwich; it is a lifestyle. It recalls steamy summer luncheon meals eaten on the terrace of a Tuscan farmhouse with a view of the hills, and then a long afternoon nap.

Preparation time: 10 minutes
Storage: None
Serves 4

8 thick slices of
the very best chewy
peasant bread

2 fat garlic cloves,
halved

2 vine-ripened
tomatoes, sliced

¼ cup
extra-virgin olive oil

Salt and freshly ground
pepper to taste

16 fresh basil leaves

1. Toast the bread.

2. Rub the cut sides of the garlic onto the toast.

3. Top the toast with the tomato slices and drizzle with the olive oil. Add the salt and pepper and top with the basil. Serve immediately. Alternatively, you can serve all the components on separate plates and let your guests assemble the sandwiches at the table.

Variations: There are too many to even begin. Carol Field, in her fabulous book *Italy in Small Bites,* devotes about twenty pages to bruschetta, and Michele Scicolone, in *The Antipasto Table,* twelve. I suggest buying, or at least flipping through, those two excellent books for more ideas.

Feta and Vegetable Pita Sandwiches

This is one of my favorite brown-bag lunches. The pita bread gets soaked in the dressing from the peppers during the day, and by lunchtime the whole thing is slightly oozing and delicious.

I usually use a Bulgarian feta for this sandwich. I find it to be less salty than the Greek kind.

Preparation time: 10 minutes
Storage: 1 day, well wrapped in plastic wrap and refrigerated
Serves 4

4 whole-wheat or
regular pita breads

1 cup chopped roasted
red peppers, preferably
oil-packed

1 cup sliced cucumber

1 cup sliced
green bell peppers

1 cup crumbled
feta cheese

Pinch of dried oregano

Salt and freshly ground
pepper to taste

1. Slice a small piece off the top of each pita bread to expose the interior pockets.

2. In a medium bowl, combine the roasted peppers, cucumber, bell peppers, and cheese. Add the oregano and salt and pepper, and toss well.

3. Stuff the pitas with the filling. Serve immediately or wrap in plastic and brown-bag it.

Variation: Substitute about 1 tablespoon chopped fresh oregano for the dried. Sliced red onions are a nice addition, as are olives.

pizzas, calzones, and focaccias

Focaccia with Walnuts and Blue Cheese

This full-flavored focaccia makes a nice hors d'oeuvre when served straight from the oven.

Preparation time: 10 minutes, plus baking
Storage: A few hours at room temperature
Serves 12 as an accompaniment

1 pound pizza dough, prepared or homemade (page 244)

1 cup (8 ounces) blue cheese, crumbled

1 cup coarsely chopped walnuts

2 tablespoons extra-virgin olive oil

Freshly ground pepper to taste

1. Preheat oven to 450° F. Grease a baking sheet.

2. Using a lightly floured rolling pin or floured hands, roll or press the dough into a 10 x 14-inch rectangle. Transfer to the prepared pan.

3. Scatter the blue cheese and walnuts over the dough to within 1 inch of the edges. Drizzle with the olive oil and grind the pepper over the top. Bake until the crust is golden brown, 12 to 17 minutes. Remove pan to a wire rack to cool for 5 minutes. Cut the focaccia in slices, and serve, preferably while still warm.

Variations: Substitute hazelnuts or pine nuts for the walnuts, and perhaps goat cheese or brie for the blue cheese.

Focaccia with Sun-Dried Tomatoes

Preparation time: 10 minutes, plus baking

Storage: A few hours at room temperature

Serves 12 as an accompaniment

1 pound pizza dough,
prepared or homemade
(page 244)

1 cup coarsely chopped
oil-packed sun-dried tomatoes

3 tablespoons freshly
grated Parmesan cheese

Freshly ground
pepper to taste

1. Preheat the oven to 450° F. Grease a baking sheet.

2. Using a lightly floured rolling pin or floured hands, roll or press the dough into a 10 x 14-inch rectangle. Transfer to the prepared pan.

3. Scatter the sun-dried tomatoes over the dough to within 1 inch of the edges. Sprinkle with the Parmesan and grind the pepper on top. Bake until the crust is golden brown, 12 to 17 minutes. Remove the pan to a wire rack to cool for 5 minutes. Cut focaccia in slices, and serve, preferably while still warm.

Focaccia Stuffed with Roasted Garlic and Basil

Preparation time: 20 minutes, plus baking

Storage: A few hours at room temperature

Serves 8–10 as an accompaniment

1 pound pizza dough, prepared or homemade (page 244)

2 heads Roasted Garlic (page 231), separated into cloves and peeled

3 tablespoons freshly grated Parmesan cheese

¼ cup chopped fresh basil

2 tablespoons extra-virgin olive oil

Salt and freshly ground pepper to taste

1. Preheat the oven to 450° F. Grease a baking sheet.

2. Using a lightly floured rolling pin or floured hands, roll or press the dough into a 10 x 14-inch rectangle. Transfer to the prepared pan.

3. Scatter the roasted garlic over the dough to within 1 inch of the edges. Sprinkle with the Parmesan and basil, then drizzle with the olive oil and add the salt and pepper. Picking up one of the short sides, fold the dough in half. It should now measure 10 x 7. Roll or pat the dough into a 10-inch square.

4. Bake until the crust is golden brown, 15 to 20 minutes. Remove pan to a wire rack to cool for 5 minutes. Cut the focaccia in slices, and serve, preferably while still warm.

Variations: Add ½ cup chopped pitted olives or oil-packed sun-dried tomatoes along with the garlic.

Focaccia Stuffed with Fresh Herbs and Olive Oil

Use a combination of herbs for this fragrant focaccia. I particularly favor a combination of thyme, chervil, and chives, although basil and marjoram are a close second.

Preparation time: 20 minutes, plus baking
Storage: A few hours at room temperature
Serves 12 as an accompaniment

1 pound pizza dough, prepared or homemade (page 244)	**2 tablespoons extra-virgin olive oil**
1 cup chopped fresh herbs	**Salt and freshly ground pepper to taste**

1. Preheat the oven to 450° F. Grease a baking sheet.

2. Using a lightly floured rolling pin or floured hands, roll or press the dough into a 10 x 14-inch rectangle. Transfer to the prepared pan.

3. Scatter the herbs over the dough, then drizzle with the olive oil and add the salt and pepper. Pick up one of the short sides and fold the dough in half. It should now measure 10 x 7. Roll or pat the dough into a 10-inch square.

4. Bake until the crust is golden brown, 15 to 20 minutes. Remove the pan to a wire rack to cool for 5 minutes. Cut the focaccia in slices, and serve, preferably while still warm.

Pesto Focaccia

While I was writing this book, a friend of mine asked me if I could get through a single chapter without using pesto in any of the recipes. Does the dessert chapter count?

Preparation time: 10 minutes, plus baking
Storage: A few hours at room temperature
Serves 12 as an accompaniment

1 pound pizza dough,
prepared or homemade
(page 244)

¾ cup pesto,
prepared or homemade
(page 234)

Salt and freshly ground
pepper to taste

1. Preheat the oven to 450° F. Grease a baking sheet.

2. Using a lightly floured rolling pin or floured hands, roll or press the dough into a 10 x 14-inch rectangle. Transfer to the prepared pan.

3. Spread the dough with the pesto, leaving a ¼-inch border. Add the salt and pepper.

4. Bake until the crust is golden brown, 12 to 17 minutes. Remove the pan to a wire rack to cool for 5 minutes. Cut the focaccia in slices, and serve, preferably while still warm.

Variations: Paper-thin slices of a ripe tomato taste delicious on this focaccia. Add them before baking.

Focaccia with Three Onions

Preparation time: 20 minutes, plus baking

Storage: A few hours at room temperature

Serves 12 as an accompaniment

1 pound pizza dough,
prepared or homemade
(page 244)

2 tablespoons
extra-virgin olive oil

1 large red onion, sliced

1 large Spanish
onion, sliced

4 scallions,
trimmed and sliced

Pinch of dried thyme

1 tablespoon balsamic
or sherry vinegar

Salt and freshly ground
pepper to taste

1. Preheat the oven to 450° F. Grease a baking sheet.

2. Using a lightly floured rolling pin or floured hands, roll or press the dough into a 10 x 14-inch rectangle. Transfer to the prepared pan. Cover dough with plastic wrap and let it rest while you prepare the topping.

3. In a large skillet, heat the olive oil over medium heat. Add the onions, scallions, and thyme and sauté until they are tender, 6 to 7 minutes. Stir in the vinegar, salt, and pepper.

4. Scatter the onions over the dough. Bake until the crust is golden brown, 12 to 17 minutes. Remove pan to a wire rack to cool for 5 minutes. Cut the focaccia in slices, and serve, preferably while still warm.

Variations: Top this pizza with about ½ cup Swiss or gruyère cheese, and add black olives, which I don't bother pitting.

Pancetta, Pearl Onion, and Sage Pizza

I love frozen pearl onions; they really make this simple pizza a show stopper.

Preparation time: 20 minutes, plus baking
Storage: Topping keeps 2 days refrigerated
Serves 4

1 pound pizza dough,
prepared or homemade
(page 244)

1 tablespoon olive oil

6 ounces pancetta,
chopped

3 cups frozen
pearl onions, thawed

1 teaspoon sugar

¼ cup chopped
fresh sage leaves,
or 3 tablespoons dried

3 tablespoons balsamic
vinegar

Salt and freshly ground
pepper to taste

1. Preheat the oven to 450° F. Grease a baking sheet.

2. Using a lightly floured rolling pin or floured hands, roll or press the dough into a 10 x 14-inch rectangle. Transfer to the prepared pan. Cover dough with plastic wrap and let rise while you prepare the topping.

3. In a large skillet over medium heat, combine the oil and pancetta. Cook until the pancetta is translucent, about 2 minutes. Add the onions and sugar, and cook, stirring, over high heat, until the onions are lightly browned and caramelized, about 5 minutes. Stir in the sage, vinegar, salt, and pepper and remove from the heat.

4. Spread the onion mixture over the dough to within $\frac{1}{2}$ inch of the edges. Bake the pizza until the crust is golden, 15 to 20 minutes.

Classic Pizza with Tomatoes, Basil, and Mozzarella

It's important to use a chunky tomato sauce for this pizza. If you are stuck with the smooth kind, however, adding a few chopped tomatoes will improve the texture.

Preparation time: 10 minutes, plus baking
Storage: None
Serves 4

1 pound pizza dough, prepared or homemade (page 244)

2 cups Chunky Fresh Tomato Sauce (page 241)

10 fresh basil leaves

2 cups shredded or thinly sliced mozzarella, preferably fresh

3 tablespoons freshly grated Parmesan cheese

Salt and freshly ground pepper to taste

1. Preheat the oven to 450° F. Grease a baking sheet.

2. Using a lightly floured rolling pin or floured hands, roll or press the dough into a 10 x 14-inch rectangle. Transfer to the prepared pan.

3. Spread the tomato sauce over the dough to within $\frac{1}{2}$ inch of the edges. Decorate with the basil leaves, then top with the cheeses, salt, and pepper. Bake the pizza until the crust is golden, 15 to 20 minutes.

Variations: Olives, sun-dried tomatoes, shredded prosciutto, and roasted or lightly sautéed garlic are all nice additions. For a slight bite, drizzle the baked pizza with hot pepper oil before serving.

Portobello and Parmesan Pizza

The portobello mushrooms add a wonderful meatiness to this otherwise simple preparation.

Preparation time: 20 minutes, plus baking
Storage: Topping keeps 2 days refrigerated
Serves 4

1 pound pizza dough,
prepared or homemade
(page 244)

2 tablespoons
extra-virgin olive oil

4 garlic cloves, minced

1/2 pound portobello
mushrooms, cleaned
and sliced

2 tablespoons chopped
fresh basil

Salt and freshly ground
pepper to taste

1/2 cup freshly
grated Parmesan cheese

1. Preheat the oven to 450° F. Grease a baking sheet.

2. Using a lightly floured rolling pin or floured hands, roll or press the dough into a 10 x 14-inch rectangle. Transfer to the prepared pan. Cover dough with plastic wrap and let rise while you prepare the topping.

3. In a large skillet over medium heat, heat the oil. Add the garlic and mushrooms and sauté until the mushrooms are soft, about 6 minutes. Stir in the basil, salt, and pepper.

4. Spread the mushroom mixture over the dough to within 1/2 inch of the edges. Top with the cheese. Bake the pizza until the crust is golden, 15 to 20 minutes.

Variations: Sliced red onions can be sautéed along with the mushrooms.

Olivada and Ricotta Pizza with Fresh Tomatoes and Garlic

I love the way the salty olivada is mellowed by the creamy ricotta cheese in this pizza. Serve it with a robust red wine.

Preparation time: 10 minutes, plus baking
Storage: None
Serves 4

1 pound pizza dough, prepared or homemade (page 244)

1½ cups ricotta cheese

½ cup green or black olivada, prepared or homemade (page 233)

2 garlic cloves, minced

¼ cup chopped fresh basil

2 large ripe tomatoes, thinly sliced and seeded

1 tablespoon olive oil

1. Preheat the oven to 450° F. Grease a baking sheet.

2. Using a lightly floured rolling pin or floured hands, roll or press the dough into a 10 x 14-inch rectangle. Transfer to the prepared pan.

3. In a small bowl, combine the ricotta cheese, olivada, garlic, and basil.

4. Spread the ricotta mixture over the dough to within ½ inch of the edges. Top with the tomatoes and drizzle the olive oil on top. Bake the pizza until the crust is golden, 15 to 20 minutes.

Roasted Red and Yellow Pepper Pizza with Goat Cheese

Preparation time: 10 minutes, plus baking

Storage: None

Serves 4

1 pound pizza dough,
prepared or homemade
(page 244)

1 cup sliced roasted
red and yellow peppers

1 cup crumbled goat cheese
(about 4 ounces)

¼ cup chopped
fresh mint

2 tablespoons
extra-virgin olive oil

1. Preheat the oven to 450° F. Grease a baking sheet.

2. Using a lightly floured rolling pin or floured hands, roll or press the dough into a 10 x 14-inch rectangle. Transfer to the prepared pan.

3. Scatter the peppers and cheese over the dough, leaving a ½-inch border. Bake the pizza until the crust is golden, 15 to 20 minutes. Top with the mint and drizzle with the olive oil before serving.

Variations: Other herbs can be substituted for the mint, and other cheeses for the goat cheese.

Shrimp and Pesto Pizza with Tomatoes

A stunning and delicious combination of green-flecked pesto, pearly pinkish shrimp, and red tomatoes.

Preparation time: 10 minutes, plus baking
Storage: None
Serves 4

1 pound pizza dough, prepared or homemade (page 244)

1 cup pesto, prepared or homemade (page 234)

1 pound large shrimp, shelled

Pinch of hot red pepper flakes, or to taste

2 cups thinly sliced ripe tomatoes

2 tablespoons extra-virgin olive oil

1. Preheat the oven to 450° F. Grease a baking sheet.

2. Using a lightly floured rolling pin or floured hands, roll or press the dough into a 10 x 14-inch rectangle. Transfer to the prepared pan.

3. In a small bowl, combine the pesto, shrimp, and red pepper flakes.

4. Top the dough with the tomatoes and drizzle on the olive oil. Top with the pesto-coated shrimp. Bake the pizza until the crust is golden and the shrimp are pink, 15 to 20 minutes.

Variations: For Scallop and Pesto Pizza with Tomatoes, substitute bay scallops or quartered sea scallops for the shrimp.

Cumin-Scented Chickpea and Vegetable Pizza

Think salad bar when you consider this pizza. The vegetables I listed are just suggestions; use whatever are cut and calling to you.

Preparation time: 15 minutes, plus baking
Storage: None
Serves 4

1 pound pizza dough, prepared or homemade (page 244)

2 tablespoons extra-virgin olive oil

1 teaspoon cumin seeds

1 cup cubed seeded tomatoes

½ cup frozen corn kernels

1 cup canned chickpeas, rinsed

½ cup thinly sliced zucchini

1 cup sliced white mushrooms

Salt and freshly ground pepper to taste

1. Preheat the oven to 450° F. Grease a baking sheet.

2. Using a lightly floured rolling pin or floured hands, roll or press the dough into a 10 x 14-inch rectangle. Transfer to the prepared pan.

3. Heat the olive oil over high heat until it is hot but not smoking. Add the cumin seeds and turn off the heat.

4. Scatter the vegetables over the dough, leaving a ½-inch border. Drizzle with the olive oil mixture and add the salt and pepper. Bake the pizza until the crust is golden, 15 to 20 minutes.

Variations: Substitute canned kidney beans or frozen lima beans for the chickpeas.

Watercress Pizza

This dish is like a salad on a pizza. I love biting into the slightly wilted peppery watercress leaves on top of the hot, cheesy pizza.

Preparation time: 15 minutes, plus baking
Storage: None
Serves 4

1 pound pizza dough, prepared or homemade (page 244)

1 cup chunky tomato sauce, prepared or homemade (page 241)

1 cup grated mozzarella, preferably fresh

⅓ cup freshly grated Parmesan cheese

2 cups (1 bunch) watercress leaves, washed

1 tablespoon extra-virgin olive oil

Salt and freshly ground pepper to taste

1. Preheat the oven to 450° F. Grease a baking sheet.

2. Using a lightly floured rolling pin or floured hands, roll or press the dough into a 10 x 14-inch rectangle. Transfer to the prepared pan.

3. Spread the tomato sauce over the dough, leaving a ½-inch border. Sprinkle on the cheese. Bake the pizza until the crust is golden, 15 to 20 minutes. Top with the watercress and drizzle on the olive oil. Sprinkle with salt and pepper.

White Bean and Mint Pizza

This unusual pizza has found many fans among my friends. Serve it with a cucumber salad.

Preparation time: 15 minutes
Storage: Topping keeps 2 days refrigerated
Serves 4

1 pound pizza dough,
prepared or homemade
(page 244)

$\frac{1}{4}$ cup extra-virgin olive oil

4 garlic cloves, minced

1 can (16 ounces)
white beans, rinsed

$\frac{1}{3}$ cup chopped fresh mint

Salt and freshly ground
pepper to taste

1. Preheat the oven to 450° F. Grease a baking sheet.

2. Using a lightly floured rolling pin or floured hands, roll or press the dough into a 10 x 14-inch rectangle. Transfer to the prepared pan.

3. Heat the olive oil over medium-low heat until it is hot but not smoking. Add the garlic and sauté until it is opaque, about 1 minute. Stir in the white beans and the mint.

4. Spread the bean mixture over the dough, leaving a $\frac{1}{2}$-inch border. Add the salt and pepper. Bake the pizza until the crust is golden, 15 to 20 minutes.

Variations: Add 1 cup chopped roasted red peppers for a wonderfully juicy texture and a gorgeous color. Other herbs can be substituted for the mint. I also like to use basil and chervil. Sometime I add a thinly sliced red onion to the top before baking.

Beet, Blue Cheese, and Chive Pizza

If you have used fresh baby beets and have the tender beet greens, make them into a salad to serve alongside.

Preparation time: 10 minutes, plus baking
Storage: None
Serves 4

1 pound pizza dough, prepared or homemade (page 244)

2 cups sliced cooked beets (canned, frozen, or fresh)

1 cup (about 4 ounces) crumbled blue cheese

2 tablespoons olive oil

Freshly ground pepper to taste

$\frac{1}{3}$ cup chopped fresh chives

1. Preheat the oven to 450° F. Grease a baking sheet.

2. Using a lightly floured rolling pin or floured hands, roll or press the dough into a 10 x 14-inch rectangle. Transfer to the prepared pan.

3. Spread the beets over the dough, leaving a $\frac{1}{2}$-inch border. Scatter on the blue cheese. Drizzle on the olive oil and grind on the pepper. Bake the pizza until the crust is golden, 15 to 20 minutes. Serve garnished with the chives.

Variations: Add up to $\frac{1}{2}$ cup toasted walnuts, pecans, or hazelnuts. The crunch is very satisfying.

Smoked Turkey–Spinach Calzone

I got the idea for this recipe at the farmers' market in New York's Union Square. One stand always has large smoked turkey drumsticks for sale.

Preparation time: 20 minutes, plus baking
Storage: Filling keeps 2 days refrigerated
Serves 2–4

1 pound pizza dough, prepared or homemade (page 244)

2 tablespoons extra-virgin olive oil

2 garlic cloves, minced

½ cup diced tomato

1 package (10 ounces) frozen chopped spinach, thawed

Salt and freshly ground pepper to taste

Freshly grated nutmeg to taste

1 teaspoon balsamic vinegar

4 ounces smoked turkey, cut into 1-inch cubes

½ cup grated mozzarella cheese

1. Preheat the oven to 450° F. Grease a baking sheet.

2. Punch down the dough. Using a lightly floured rolling pin or floured hands, roll the dough into a 12-inch circle. Transfer the dough to the prepared pan.

3. Prepare the filling: In a large skillet over medium-high heat, heat the olive oil. Add the garlic and sauté for 30 seconds. Add the tomato and spinach and cook until most of the liquid has evaporated, 5 to 8 minutes. Using a slotted spoon, remove the mixture to a medium bowl. Add the salt, pepper, nutmeg, and balsamic vinegar.

4. Add the smoked turkey and mozzarella to the spinach mixture, stirring to combine. Spread the mixture evenly over half the dough to within 1 inch of the edge. Fold the unfilled side over the filling and pinch the edges to seal. Prick the top with a fork. Bake the calzone until golden brown, 15 to 20 minutes. Serve immediately.

Bite-Sized Pizzas

I like to make these small pizzas for a cocktail party. I have all the topping ingredients ready, and I just assemble them as the party continues.

Preparation time: 10 minutes per batch, plus baking
Storage: None
Serves 10–14 as an hors d'oeuvre

1 pound pizza dough, prepared or homemade (page 244)

4 cups any toppings or combination from other pizza recipes

$\frac{1}{3}$ cup extra-virgin olive oil

1. Preheat the oven to 450° F. Grease several baking sheets. Punch the dough down. Divide the dough into 16 or more equal pieces. Using floured hands, pat each piece into a 2-inch disk and arrange the disks 2 inches apart on the prepared pans. Spoon some of the desired topping on the dough and drizzle with the olive oil.

2. Bake the pizzas until the crust is golden brown, 8 to 12 minutes. Serve immediately.

Suggested toppings: Roasted red peppers, sun-dried tomatoes, olives, olivada, pesto, grated or crumbled cheeses, nuts, onions, garlic sautéed in olive oil, roasted garlic, vegetables, shrimp, scallops, squid, caramelized onions, anchovies, pepperoni, prosciutto, crumbled bacon, tomato sauce, fresh herbs, or any combination of the above.

pasta and polenta

Wild Mushroom Linguine

In addition to pasta, this versatile sauce can be used on almost anything crying out to be sauced: pasta, polenta, sautéed chicken, beef, or veal. Try it as a topping for vegetables, such as fresh or frozen green beans, artichoke hearts, or spinach. It also freezes well.

Woodland Pantry has a fabulous wild mushroom powder that adds a tremendous boost to almost everything. If you can't find it in your grocery store, it is available by mail order (see Sources, page vi).

Preparation time: 20 minutes
Storage: 3 days refrigerated, 2 months frozen
Serves 6

1 pound linguine

2 tablespoons
extra-virgin olive oil

2 garlic cloves, minced

1 pound white mushrooms,
sliced (or 2 packages
frozen mushrooms)

1 teaspoon dried
wild mushroom powder

2 cups heavy cream

⅓ cup finely
chopped fresh basil

Salt and freshly ground
pepper to taste

Freshly grated
Parmesan cheese to taste

1. Cook the linguine according to the package directions.

2. Meanwhile, in a large skillet over medium-low heat, heat the olive oil until it is hot but not smoking. Add the garlic and stir well.

3. Immediately add the mushroom slices to the pan. Sauté for about 2 minutes, until they begin to give off their juices, and then add the wild mushroom powder. Stir well.

4. Continue to sauté the mushrooms until most of the moisture evaporates, about 2 more minutes. Then add the cream and stir constantly.

5. Simmer the mixture until the cream reduces and the sauce thickens, about 5 minutes. Stir in the basil and salt and pepper. Serve immediately over pasta, with Parmesan cheese.

Parmesan Tortellini in a Bourbon-Spiked Winter Squash Sauce

In this rich entree, frozen winter squash puree is the basis for a low-fat and utterly delicious sauce for tortellini. If you have had the foresight to thaw the squash puree ahead of time, this sauce will cook even quicker. If not, you can either thaw it in the microwave or simply let the frozen puree melt in the beef broth and garlic.

Preparation time: 20 minutes
Storage: Sauce keeps 4 days refrigerated
Serves 4

1 pound
Parmesan-filled tortellini

1 cup beef broth

1 garlic clove, smashed

1 package (10 ounces)
frozen winter squash puree

2 tablespoons bourbon

1 tablespoon lemon juice

1 teaspoon fresh thyme
or a generous pinch of dried

Freshly ground
pepper and salt to taste

Freshly grated
Parmesan cheese (optional)

1. Cook the tortellini according to the package directions.

2. Meanwhile, in a small saucepan over medium heat, combine the broth, garlic, and winter squash puree. Cook the mixture, stirring, until the puree thickens a bit, 4 to 6 minutes. Stir in the bourbon, lemon juice, thyme, and salt and pepper to taste, and let simmer for 1 more minute. Remove from the heat and fish out the garlic.

3. Drain the tortellini and serve with the sauce on top. Pass the cheese, if desired.

Variations: For a spicy note, add a few gratings of nutmeg and a dash of allspice. In winter, a bay leaf adds its own distinctive perfume. A tablespoon or two of butter added at the end will enrich this sauce wonderfully, although it will no longer be so low in fat.

Porcini Tortellini with Duck Liver Mousse and Chives

Duck liver mousse, an extremely smooth and light version of pâté, forms the basis of this sauce. It is an extremely decadent combination, and is best served in small portions as an appetizer. If you cannot find tortellini filled with porcini mushrooms, use regular mushroom or vegetable tortellini.

Preparation time: 15 minutes
Storage: None
Serves 6–8 as an appetizer

1 pound porcini-stuffed tortellini	**Salt and freshly ground pepper**
6 ounces duck liver mousse	**Fresh lemon juice, if needed**
½ cup heavy cream	**⅓ cup chopped fresh chives**
3 teaspoons Cognac	

1. Cook the tortellini according to package directions.

2. Meanwhile, prepare the sauce: In a small saucepan over low heat, combine the duck liver mousse and cream. Cook the mixture, stirring constantly, until it is smooth. Stir in the Cognac and cook 1 minute longer. Remove the pan from the heat and stir in the salt, pepper, and lemon juice, if desired.

3. Toss the tortellini with the sauce and serve immediately, garnished with the chives.

Wagon Wheels with Tuna, Tomatoes, and Mint

For best flavor, use tuna packed in olive-oil from Italy for this lusty dish. Tossing the hot pasta with the cold sauce helps melt the butter and creates a wonderful contrast.

Preparation time: 15 minutes
Storage: Tuna mixture keeps 12 hours in the refrigerator
Serves 2–3

1 pound wagon wheels	2 tablespoons chopped fresh mint
1 can (6 to 7 ounces) tuna, drained	2 large ripe tomatoes, diced
¼ cup extra-virgin olive oil	3 tablespoons butter
2 tablespoons lemon juice	Salt and freshly ground pepper to taste

1. Cook the wagon wheels according to the package directions.

2. While the pasta is cooking, combine the tuna, olive oil, lemon juice, and mint in a small bowl, breaking up the tuna with a fork.

3. Drain the pasta and place it in a large bowl. Mix it with the tomatoes and the butter, tossing until the butter melts.

4. Add the tuna mixture and toss to combine. Taste and add salt and pepper.

Variations: For added piquancy, add any or all of the following: 1 to 2 chopped garlic cloves, 1 tablespoon drained capers, 3 tablespoons chopped red onion. Furthermore, colorful vegetables add texture and flavor; add up to 1 cup of any of the following: diced red or yellow peppers, cooked peas, corn kernels, cubed cucumber, and/or diced avocado.

Instant Lasagna

Here is a happy surprise for the lasagna lover: you need not cook the lasagna noodles before assembling the dish! Soaking them in hot water before forming the layers is enough to ensure the pasta is cooked through but not mushy.

Preparation time: 15 minutes plus baking
Storage: 4 days refrigerated, 3 months frozen
Serves 8–10

1 package lasagna noodles

2 containers (15 ounces each) ricotta cheese

2 eggs

½ cup grated Parmesan cheese

Freshly ground pepper to taste

2 quarts good tomato sauce

2 cups (about 1 pound) grated mozzarella cheese

1. Preheat the oven to 375° F. In a large bowl or a sink filled with hot water, soak the lasagna noodles while you prepare the filling.

2. Mix the ricotta cheese, eggs, Parmesan cheese, and pepper until smooth. Set aside.

3. Pour a thin layer of tomato sauce on the bottom of a 12 x 15-inch baking pan. Tilt the pan to make sure the sauce covers the entire surface. Place one layer of lasagna noodles on top of the sauce. Do not dry them before placing them in the pan; the water still clinging will help them cook.

4. Cover the noodles with another thin layer of sauce, then spoon half of the ricotta mixture over it. Top the ricotta with ½ cup of mozzarella cheese, then another layer of sauce, then more noodles, sauce, the rest of the ricotta, another ½ cup of moz-

zarella, and the final layer of noodles. Top the final layer of noodles with the remaining sauce and then the mozzarella cheese.

5. Cover the baking dish with foil and bake for 35 minutes. Remove the foil and continue baking until the cheese is melted and the sauce bubbling, 10 to 15 minutes more. Remove the lasagna from the oven and let sit for 10 minutes to set before serving.

Variations: For Vegetable Lasagna, add a layer of sautéed spinach, mushrooms, or broccoli, or some fried or baked eggplant slices. For Red Pepper Lasagna, use a red pepper–flavored tomato sauce (such as Progresso), and layer with jarred or canned roasted red peppers. For Pesto Lasagna, add 1 cup pesto to the ricotta mixture, then garnish the dish with fresh basil leaves.

Penne with Ground Veal and Radicchio

This extremely pretty dish is almost a meal in itself.

Preparation time: 15 minutes
Storage: None
Serves 4

1 pound penne

2 tablespoons
extra-virgin olive oil

3 garlic cloves, minced

¾ pound ground veal

Salt and freshly ground
pepper to taste

½ cup heavy cream

1 small head radicchio,
washed, cored,
and chopped

1 tablespoon grated
lemon peel

Freshly grated
Parmesan cheese

1. Cook the pasta according to the package directions.

2. While the pasta is cooking, make the sauce. In a large skillet, heat the olive oil over medium heat until it is hot but not smoking. Add the garlic and sauté until it just turns opaque, about 30 seconds. Add the veal and sauté, breaking up the pieces so it browns evenly, about 5 minutes. Add the salt and pepper.

3. Pour the cream into the skillet and cook until it thickens, about 2 minutes. Stir in the radicchio and lemon peel.

4. Serve the pasta with the sauce on top and pass the Parmesan cheese.

Variations: For a lighter dish, substitute broth or white wine for the cream. To make Pasta with Ground Veal and Scallions, substitute 3 scallions for the garlic and omit the radicchio. Of course, you can always add garlic in addition to the scallions.

Black Pepper Pasta with Ricotta Salata

Preparation time: 15 minutes
Storage: None
Serves 4–6

1 pound linguine	2 cups grated or crumbled ricotta salata
¼ cup extra-virgin olive oil	2 teaspoons coarsely ground pepper, or to taste

1. Cook the pasta according to the package directions.

2. Drain the pasta and toss it with the olive oil, cheese, and black pepper. Serve immediately.

Variations: For Black Pepper Pasta with Goat Cheese and Arugula, simply substitute a flavorful goat cheese (such as Bucheron) for the ricotta salata, and add 1 bunch (2 cups) chopped arugula leaves. This is a good place to use flavored olive oils that can be so wonderful. I like this dish with tarragon oil, but oregano or basil are delightful as well. A few chopped ripe plum tomatoes are also lovely and add a juicy contrast to the creamy cheese.

Fettuccine with Red Onion, Cilantro, and Smoked Trout

Although I generally serve this hot, it is also delicious at room temperature, making it a good buffet pasta (a rare thing!).

Preparation time: 15 minutes
Storage: 1 hour if serving at room temperature
Serves 4–6

1 pound fettuccine

½ cup extra-virgin olive oil

1 small red onion, thinly sliced

½ cup chopped fresh cilantro

¼ pound smoked trout, flaked

Salt and freshly ground pepper to taste

1 teaspoon grated lemon zest

1. Cook the pasta according to the package directions.

2. While the pasta is cooking, make the sauce. In a large skillet, heat the olive oil until it is hot but not smoking. Add the onion and sauté over medium-low heat until it begins to wilt, about 4 minutes. Add the cilantro and remove from the heat.

3. Drain the pasta and toss it with the onion mixture. Add the trout, salt, pepper, and lemon zest and toss to combine. Serve immediately or at room temperature.

Variations: To make Pasta with Basil and Smoked Trout, replace the onion with 2 minced garlic cloves and the cilantro with fresh basil. You may or may not want to omit the lemon in this version.

Pasta with Hazelnuts, Crème Fraîche, and Sage

I prefer a denser, meatier pasta such as orecchiette, shells, or wagon wheels for this dish.

Preparation time: 15 minutes
Storage: Sauce keeps 1 day refrigerated
Serves 4–6

1 pound pasta

2 garlic cloves, minced

1 cup toasted hazelnuts

½ cup crème fraîche or sour cream

Salt and freshly ground pepper to taste

1 tablespoon chopped fresh sage

⅓ cup freshly grated Parmesan cheese

1. Cook the pasta according to the package directions.

2. Meanwhile, make the sauce: In a food processor fitted with a steel blade or a blender, process the garlic, nuts, and crème fraîche until smooth. Add salt and pepper.

3. Drain the pasta and toss with the sauce. Top with the sage and cheese and serve immediately.

Variations: For Pistachio Cream Pasta, simply substitute roasted pistachio nuts for the hazelnuts, and cream for the crème fraîche. Omit the sage.

Gnocchi with Olives, Tomatoes, and Arugula

I like to use Moroccan olives for this dish; they are easy to pit and have a nice, briny flavor.

Preparation time: 20 minutes
Storage: None
Serves 4

1 pound gnocchi

¼ cup extra-virgin olive oil

Juice of 1 lemon

Pinch of hot red pepper flakes (optional)

2 large bunches arugula (3–4 cups), washed and chopped

½ cup pitted black olives

6 ripe plum tomatoes, cut into ½-inch cubes

Salt to taste

Freshly grated Parmesan cheese (optional)

1. Bring a large pot of salted water to a boil. Add the gnocchi and boil until it is cooked through, about 3 to 6 minutes.

2. Meanwhile, make the sauce: In a large skillet, heat the olive oil over low heat until it is hot but not smoking. Remove the pan from the heat and stir in the lemon juice and red pepper flakes, if desired.

3. In a large bowl, combine the oil mixture, arugula, olives, tomatoes, and salt. Drain the gnocchi and toss it with the arugula mixture. Serve with Parmesan cheese.

Variations: Gently heat 1 or 2 minced garlic cloves with the olive oil. Capers can be substituted for the olives, as can chopped sun-dried tomatoes.

Fusilli with Artichokes and Wine

Frozen artichoke hearts are a wonderful ingredient to keep on hand; using them instead of fresh ones cuts down the labor in this savory dish.

Preparation time: 15 minutes
Storage: Sauce keeps up to 2 hours at room temperature
Serves 4

1 pound fusilli

3 tablespoons butter

4 garlic cloves, minced

2 packages (10 ounces each) frozen quartered artichoke hearts, thawed

1¼ cups dry white wine

1 tablespoon chopped fresh parsley

Salt and freshly ground pepper to taste

Freshly grated Parmesan cheese (optional)

1. Cook the pasta according to the package directions.

2. Meanwhile, prepare the sauce: In a large skillet, melt the butter over medium heat. Add the garlic and the artichokes and sauté until the artichokes are tender, about 3 minutes. Add the wine and cook the mixture until the wine is evaporated by

about half, 2 to 3 minutes. Remove pan from heat and stir in the parsley, salt, and pepper. (If holding over, reheat just before serving.)

3. Drain the pasta and toss it with the sauce. Serve with Parmesan cheese, if desired.

Variations: For Fusilli with Artichokes and Prosciutto, add about $\frac{1}{4}$ pound slivered imported prosciutto to the sauce just before serving. For added oomph, make Fusilli with Artichokes and Anchovies by adding 2 or 3 mashed anchovy fillets (or a tablespoon of anchovy paste) to the artichokes with the wine.

Linguine with Gorgonzola, Pine Nuts, and Watercress

Although sweet gorgonzola is the blue cheese of choice for this piquant dish, you can substitute other types, such as bleu de Bresse or Stilton, with excellent if less Italian results. Toasted almonds can be substituted for the pine nuts.

Preparation time: 15 minutes
Storage: None
Serves 4–6

1 pound fresh linguine

$1\frac{1}{4}$ cups crumbled sweet gorgonzola (Dolcelatte)

1 cup heavy cream

Freshly ground pepper to taste

$\frac{1}{3}$ cup toasted pine nuts

2 cups (about 1 bunch) watercress, stemmed and washed

1. Cook the linguine according to the package directions.

2. Meanwhile, prepare the sauce: In a small saucepan over low heat, combine the cheese and the cream. Cook the mixture, stirring, until the cheese just melts.

3. Drain the pasta and toss it with the cheese mixture, pepper, and pine nuts. Serve immediately, garnished with the watercress.

Egg Pasta with Corn and Lump Crab Meat

If you don't want to bother with both the basil and the mint, simply choose one.

Preparation time: 15 minutes
Storage: None
Serves 4–6

1 pound egg pasta	Salt and freshly ground pepper to taste
5 tablespoons extra-virgin olive oil	2 tablespoons chopped fresh basil
1 package (about 10 ounces) frozen sweet corn kernels	2 tablespoons chopped fresh mint
1 pound lump crab meat, picked over	

1. Cook the pasta according to the package directions.

2. Meanwhile, prepare the sauce: In a large skillet, heat the olive oil over low heat. Add the corn kernels and cook until they are defrosted, 1 to 2 minutes. Remove the pan from the heat and stir in the crab meat.

3. Drain the pasta and toss it with the crab mixture. Add the salt and pepper and serve immediately, garnished with the basil and mint.

Variations: In tomato season, I like to serve this dish with chopped fresh tomatoes. Chopped sweet green and red peppers are nice when sautéed in the olive oil before adding the corn. Substituting cilantro for the mint is also a nice exchange.

Green Olivada Pasta

This incredibly easy dish is just the thing to serve in winter, when all flavors begin to pale and the appetite wanes.

Preparation time: 15 minutes
Storage: None
Serves 4–6

1 pound spaghetti
or other pasta

1 cup green olivada,
prepared or homemade
(page 238)

Juice of ½ lemon

1 tablespoon fresh
thyme leaves,
or 1 teaspoon dried

Freshly ground
pepper to taste

Freshly ground
Parmesan cheese (optional)

1. Cook the pasta according to the package directions.

2. Drain the pasta and toss with the olivada, lemon juice, and thyme. Add the freshly ground pepper and serve with Parmesan cheese, if desired.

Fresh Pasta with Salmon Caviar and Smoked Salmon

Sometimes I like to use fresh spinach fettuccine in this amazingly simple preparation.

Preparation time: 15 minutes
Storage: None
Serves 4–6

1 pound fresh fettuccine

1 cup heavy cream

¼ pound smoked
salmon, shredded

⅓ cup salmon caviar

Freshly ground
pepper to taste

1. Cook the fettuccine according to the package directions.

2. Meanwhile, heat the cream in a saucepan over medium heat until it comes to a boil. Reduce the cream until it thickens slightly, about 2 minutes.

3. Drain the pasta and toss it with the cream and smoked salmon. Serve immediately, garnished with the caviar and topped with the pepper.

Fresh Spinach Pasta with Shrimp and Creamy Pesto

Preparation time: 10 minutes
Storing: None
Serves 4–6

1 pound fresh spinach linguine or fettuccine

1 cup best-quality pesto, prepared or homemade (page 234)

⅓ cup sour cream

1 teaspoon balsamic vinegar

Salt and freshly ground pepper to taste

1 pound fresh small or medium shrimp, shelled

1. Cook the pasta according to the package directions.

2. Meanwhile, in a serving bowl, combine the pesto, sour cream, vinegar, salt, and pepper.

3. About 1 minute before the pasta is done to your taste, add the shrimp to the pot. Cook until the pasta and shrimp are both just done. Drain immediately and toss with the sauce.

Variation: For Spinach Pasta with Scallops and Creamy Pesto, substitute bay scallops or quartered sea scallops for the shrimp.

Pasta Shells with Cherry Tomatoes, Basil, and Smoked Mozzarella

In this summery dish, the heat of the pasta slightly melts the cheese and warms the tomatoes and basil, releasing their perfume. I heartily recommend using those sweet, tiny cherry tomatoes imported from Israel, which will make this a memorable dish.

Preparation time: 15 minutes, plus marinating
Storage: Sauce keeps 6 hours at room temperature
Serves 4–6

1 pint ripe cherry tomatoes, halved	2 tablespoons red wine vinegar
1 cup shredded fresh basil	2 or 3 garlic cloves, minced
¾ pound smoked mozzarella cheese, cubed	Salt and freshly ground pepper to taste
½ cup extra-virgin olive oil	1 pound pasta shells

1. At least 30 minutes before serving, combine the tomatoes, basil, cheese, olive oil, vinegar, garlic, salt, and pepper in a large serving bowl.

2. Cook pasta according to package directions. Drain and toss with the sauce.

Variations: For Pasta with Cherry Tomatoes, Basil, and Brie, substitute a ripe brie for the mozzarella. Capers, chopped anchovies, chopped onion, or olives are wonderful additions.

Polenta with Shrimp and Saffron

Make instant polenta or use the more time-consuming recipe on page 242.

Preparation time: 15 minutes
Storage: None
Serves 4 as an entree, 8 as an appetizer

1 polenta loaf in ½-inch slices	**4 tablespoons butter**
3 to 4 tablespoons extra-virgin olive oil	**1½ pounds large shrimp, shelled**
1 cup chicken broth	**3 garlic cloves, minced**
1 teaspoon saffron threads	**1 tablespoon chopped fresh parsley**

1. Preheat the grill or broiler. Brush the polenta on both sides with the olive oil. Broil or grill the polenta until it is golden brown, 2 to 3 minutes per side.

2. Meanwhile, prepare the sauce: In a small saucepan over medium heat, warm the chicken broth with the saffron until the broth comes to a bare simmer. Turn off the heat.

3. In a large skillet over medium-high heat, melt the butter. When the foam has subsided, add the shrimp and garlic and sauté until the shrimp are barely opaque but not yet cooked through, about 1 minute. Pour in the chicken broth mixture and simmer the sauce until it reduces and thickens slightly, about 2 minutes. Turn off the heat.

4. When ready to serve, arrange the polenta on a serving platter. Pour the sauce on top and garnish with the parsley. Serve immediately.

Variations: Adding 1 cup of fresh or frozen peas, or 1 cup diced young zucchini, along with the shrimp provides a wonderful color contrast in this dish.

Polenta with Avocado and Olive Oil

I love the combination of soft, ripe avocado slices against the warm, crisp polenta. Serve this dish with a tangy watercress or tomato salad for a light lunch or first course.

Preparation time: 10 minutes
Storage: None
Serves 6–8

1 polenta loaf in ½-inch slices (see Polenta, page 242)	**2 large ripe Hass avocados**
4 to 5 tablespoons extra-virgin olive oil	**Salt and freshly ground pepper to taste**

1. Preheat the grill or broiler. Brush the polenta on both sides with 3 to 4 tablespoons of the olive oil. Broil or grill the polenta until it is golden brown, 2 to 3 minutes per side.

2. Meanwhile, peel, pit, and slice the avocados.

3. When ready to serve, arrange the polenta slices on a serving platter. Top with the avocado slices, salt, and pepper, and drizzle with the remaining olive oil. Serve immediately.

Polenta with Grilled Zucchini and Basil

I like to serve this simple dish as a meatless entree, sometimes topped with grilled shrimp or scallops. However, the carnivorous set may also enjoy adding some leftover sliced steak or lamb to round out the meal.

Preparation time: 20 minutes
Storing: None
Serves 4–6

1 polenta loaf in
½-inch slices
(see Polenta, page 242)

4 or 5 small zucchini
(about 1½ pounds),
sliced lengthwise

⅓ cup extra-virgin
olive oil

1 tablespoon lemon juice

2 tablespoons chopped
fresh basil

Salt and freshly ground
pepper to taste

1. Preheat the grill or broiler. Brush the polenta and the zucchini on both sides with the olive oil. Broil or grill the polenta and zucchini until golden brown, 2 to 3 minutes per side.

2. To serve, arrange the polenta on a serving platter. Top with the zucchini and drizzle on the lemon juice. Scatter on the basil, salt, and pepper, and serve immediately.

poultry

Celeriac Juice–Poached Chicken Breasts

This recipe was inspired by Jean-George Vongerichten, the chef at JoJo and Vong in New York City. While I was in the health food store picking up beet juice and carrot juice, I also grabbed some celeriac juice. This is now one of my favorite ways to serve chicken. If you prefer not to use cream, this dish will be extremely low in fat, although the cream works out to only 1 tablespoon per person. If you plan to serve it cold (and it is delicious that way), definitely omit the cream.

Preparation time: 20 minutes
Storage: 1 day refrigerated if serving cold
Serves 4

1 bottle (12 ounces)
celeriac juice

1 garlic clove, smashed

4 skinless, boneless
chicken breast halves,
about 6 ounces each

¼ cup heavy
cream (optional)

Salt and freshly ground
pepper to taste

Freshly grated
nutmeg to taste

1. In a large skillet over low heat, bring the celeriac juice and garlic to a simmer. Add the chicken and enough water to cover them (if necessary) and keep the mixture barely simmering, adjusting the heat as necessary, for 8 to 12 minutes, or until the chicken breasts are just cooked through. Do not overcook.

2. Remove the chicken breasts to a platter and keep them warm in a 200° F. oven.

3. Raise the heat to high and boil the poaching liquid until it is reduced by two-thirds, 4 to 6 minutes. It should be thick and almost syrupy. Stir in the cream and reduce for 1 minute more. Stir in salt, pepper, and nutmeg. If serving hot, spoon the sauce over the chicken and serve immediately. Alternatively, if serving cold, let the dish return to room temperature.

Variations: Instead of cream, whisk 2 tablespoons butter into the sauce just before serving. This will thicken it and give it a lovely sheen. Fresh herbs, such as tarragon and thyme, are good additions to this dish. Walnuts or crumbled blue cheese are also nice served on top.

Citrus-Poached Chicken Breasts

Not only is this easy dish fabulous both hot and cold, it makes the very best chicken salad when tossed with a simple vinaigrette dressing and a bit of plain yogurt or mayonnaise. Serve it over arugula.

Preparation time: 15 minutes
Storage: 1 day refrigerated if serving cold
Serves 4

4 skinless, boneless
chicken breast halves,
about 6 ounces each

Salt and freshly ground
pepper

⅓ cup orange or
tangerine juice

2 tablespoons
lemon juice

1 tablespoon
lime juice

2 tablespoons
Grand Marnier

2 garlic cloves, minced

2 bay leaves

1. Preheat the oven to 375° F. Place the chicken breasts in an oiled baking pan just large enough to hold them. Pour all the citrus juices and the Grand Marnier around the chicken and scatter the garlic, bay leaves, and salt and pepper.

2. Place a piece of oiled waxed paper cut to fit inside the pan directly on top of the chicken. Bake for 8 to 10 minutes. Serve immediately, or cool and then bring to room temperature when serving cold.

Chicken with Peanut Sauce

I love the full, rich flavors in this spicy dish. If is perfect to serve to a crowd, so double or triple the recipe as needed. You can use either the yogurt or the coconut milk, just make sure the coconut milk is the unsweetened kind available at specialty markets and large supermarkets, and not cream of coconut, which is quite sweet.

Preparation time: 10 minutes
Storage: Sauce keeps 3 days refrigerated
Serves 4

2 tablespoons olive oil

4 skinless, boneless
chicken breast halves,
about 6 ounces each,
cut into 1-inch cubes

5 or 6 scallions,
trimmed, and 3 sliced

1 cup peanut sauce,
prepared or homemade
(page 232)

1 cup canned
unsweetened coconut milk
or plain yogurt

2 teaspoons soy sauce

Fresh lemon juice to taste

Hot red pepper flakes
to taste

1. In a large skillet over medium-high heat, heat the olive oil until it is hot but not smoking. Add the chicken and the sliced scallions and cook, stirring, until the chicken is cooked through and the scallions wilted, about 3 to 5 minutes.

2. Meanwhile (or ahead of time), prepare the sauce: In a small bowl, combine the peanut sauce, coconut milk, soy sauce, lemon juice, and pepper flakes. Stir well to combine.

3. Toss the chicken and scallions with the sauce before serving. Garnish with the remaining scallions, if desired.

Variations: Add 1 chopped garlic clove, 3 tablespoons chopped cilantro, or 1 tablespoon grated fresh ginger or pickled ginger to the sauce.

Chicken Brochette

You can thread colorful vegetables (which you should marinate along with the chicken) on the skewers along with the chicken.

If you use wooden skewers, don't forget to soak them in water while you marinate the chicken.

Preparation time: 10 minutes, plus marinating
Storage: Chicken marinates for up to 24 hours refrigerated
Serves 6

2 cups Herbed Vinaigrette (page 235)

2 pounds skinless, boneless chicken breasts, cut into 1½-inch cubes

1. In a flat dish or pan, combine the vinaigrette and the chicken, tossing to coat all sides. Let marinate from 15 minutes at room temperature to overnight in the refrigerator.

2. Preheat the grill or broiler. Thread chicken and whatever vegetables you want to use (if any) on metal or wooden skewers (soak wooden skewers in water). Grill or broil for 2 minutes per side. Do not overcook.

Chicken Breasts with Balsamic Vinegar

This dish is the incarnation of simplicity. Because it contains only a few ingredients, quality is paramount. Use the fruitiest, greenest olive oil you can find, the freshest free-range chicken, coarse sea salt, and aged balsamic vinegar.

Preparation time: 15 minutes
Storage: None
Serves 4

2 tablespoons extra-virgin olive oil	Salt and freshly ground pepper to taste
4 skinless, boneless chicken breast halves, about 6 ounces each	2 tablespoons balsamic vinegar

1. In a large skillet over medium-high heat, heat the olive oil until it is hot but not smoking. Add the chicken and cook until browned, 4 to 6 minutes per side.

2. Add the salt and pepper, drizzle with the balsamic vinegar, and serve at once.

Chicken in Blood Orange Sauce

I use the frozen blood orange juice imported from Italy that is currently on the market. This sauce is also terrific when served with salmon.

Preparation time: 20 minutes
Storage: None
Serves 4

2 tablespoons butter

4 skinless, boneless
chicken breast halves,
about 6 ounces each

Salt and freshly ground
pepper

1 cup blood orange juice

1 bay leaf or 2 sprigs
fresh or dried thyme

½ cup heavy cream

1. In a large skillet over medium heat, melt the butter. Add the chicken and cook until browned, 4 to 6 minutes per side. Add the salt and pepper.

2. Remove the chicken to a platter and keep it warm in a 200° F oven while you prepare the sauce.

3. Raise the heat to high. Combine the orange juice and bay leaf or thyme in the skillet and cook until reduced by half, about 5 minutes. Add the cream and cook until the sauce thickens slightly, about 3 minutes. Add salt and pepper to taste, discard the bay leaf, and serve the sauce over the chicken.

Variation: You could use regular orange juice or tangerine juice in place of the blood orange juice, but you may want to add a tablespoon of red wine vinegar to approximate its tartness.

Tandoori Chicken

This aromatic dish, based on one from Madhur Jaffrey, will have a better flavor the longer you marinate it. I usually prepare the marinade in the morning and cook the chicken in the evening, letting it rest in the refrigerator in the meantime. You can also reuse the marinade. Just freeze it until you feel like making tandoori chicken again, and the dish will be unbelievably easy.

If you have an outdoor grill, you could grill the chicken instead of roasting it. Serve it with Cumin Broccoli Salad (page 49) or with a cucumber salad, and plain rice or pita bread.

Preparation time: 20 minutes, plus marinating and roasting
Storage: Chicken marinates for up to 24 hours refrigerated.
Serves 6

2½ pounds chicken legs, skin removed	¾-inch slice fresh ginger
Salt	½ small onion, quartered
1 lemon, halved	1½ cups plain yogurt
½ jalapeño chile, or to taste	2 teaspoons garam masala
2 garlic cloves, peeled	

1. Using a small, sharp knife, make 2 slashes on each chicken leg, one on either side. The slashes should reach the bone. Rub salt and a cut lemon onto the chicken and into the slashes. Let sit while you prepare the marinade.

2. In a blender or food processor (I use a blender), blend the jalapeño, garlic, ginger, and onion until finely chopped. Add the yogurt and garam masala and blend until the mixture is smooth.

3. Place the chicken in a bowl and cover it with the marinade, making sure each piece is well coated. Cover the bowl and let the chicken marinate for at least 1 hour at room temperature and up to 24 hours in the refrigerator. The longer the better.

4. Preheat the oven to 500° F. Line a baking sheet with aluminum foil. Remove the chicken legs from the marinade and brush off any that clings. Place the chicken on the prepared pan and roast until it is just done, 20 to 25 minutes. Serve hot, cold, or at room temperature.

Variation: For an even quicker meal, buy prepared tandoori paste and mix it with yogurt. The results will be almost as delicious, and much easier.

Crispy Herbed Chicken Tenders

Chicken tenders—that is, chicken fingers cut from the breast—are easily available in most supermarkets. If you cannot find them, simply slice a chicken breast into 1-inch fingers.

Since dried herbs work so well in this flavorful dish, I always associate it with winter. Serve it on a bed of arugula or radicchio.

Preparation time: 15 minutes
Storage: None
Serves 4

1 cup unflavored
bread crumbs

1 tablespoon fresh
thyme leaves,
or 1 teaspoon dried

1 tablespoon chopped
fresh oregano, or
$\frac{1}{2}$ teaspoon dried

Pinch of fennel seeds

2 tablespoons freshly
grated Parmesan cheese

$\frac{1}{2}$ cup (1 stick)
butter, melted

Salt and freshly ground
pepper

$1\frac{1}{2}$ pounds
chicken tenders

4 to 6 tablespoons
olive oil

1. In a small, shallow bowl, combine the bread crumbs, thyme, oregano, fennel, and cheese. Mix well.

2. Place the butter, salt, and pepper in another shallow dish. Dip all the chicken pieces first into the butter, then into the bread crumb mixture.

3. In a large skillet over medium heat, heat 2 tablespoons of the olive oil until it is hot but not smoking. Add as many chicken tenders as will fit comfortably into the skillet. Cook, turning them once, until they are golden brown, 1 to 2 minutes per side. Continue with the rest of the chicken tenders, adding more olive oil to the pan as necessary. Serve immediately.

Sage Grilled Chicken with Chicken Livers

I love the varied textures in this dish. Serve it with the Hot Chickpeas Vinaigrette on page 194, and a green salad.

Preparation time: 15 minutes plus marinating
Storage: Prepared skewers keep several hours refrigerated
Serves 6–8

2 skinless, boneless chicken breast halves, cut into 1½-inch cubes

½ pound chicken livers, cleaned

2 garlic cloves, smashed

⅓ cup extra-virgin olive oil

3 tablespoons balsamic vinegar

Salt and freshly ground pepper to taste

¼ cup chopped fresh sage leaves, or 1 tablespoon dried (not powdered), crumbled

1 small baguette, sliced

1. Thread the chicken cubes and chicken livers on metal or wooden skewers (soak wooden skewers in water).

2. In a flat dish or pan, combine the garlic, olive oil, balsamic vinegar, salt, pepper, and sage. Add the skewers and turn them in the marinade to coat all sides. Let marinate from 15 minutes at room temperature to overnight in the refrigerator.

3. Preheat the grill or broiler. Spear the bread slices onto the skewers. Grill or broil for 2 to 3 minutes per side. Do not overcook. Serve immediately.

Variations: Cherry tomatoes or cubed zucchini can be threaded on the skewers with the chicken and chicken livers.

Chicken Breasts with Calvados

If you have the inclination, you can add one or two small sliced apples with the chicken. If you don't have any Calvados on hand, substitute Cognac or Armagnac.

Preparation time: 15 minutes
Storage: None
Serves 4

4 tablespoons butter

4 skinless, boneless
chicken breast halves,
6 ounces each

Salt and freshly ground
pepper to taste

4 tablespoons Calvados

$\frac{2}{3}$ cup heavy cream

1. In a large skillet over medium heat, melt the butter. Add the chicken and cook until browned, about 4 minutes per side. Add the salt and pepper.

2. Pour the Calvados into the skillet and cook until the alcohol is burned off, about 1 minute. (You could, if you are in a dramatic mood, ignite the Calvados with a match and let the flames die down.)

3. Add the cream and cook until the sauce thickens slightly, 2 to 3 minutes. Serve immediately.

Chicken with Marsala, Raisins, and Pine Nuts

Although I like the rich, dark chicken thigh meat with this slightly sweet sauce, you could use chicken breasts instead. Just lessen the cooking time appropriately.

Preparation time: 20 minutes
Storage: None
Serves 4

8 chicken thighs, skin removed	1 cup dry white wine
3 tablespoons butter	½ cup Marsala
¼ cup Cognac	Pinch of ground cinnamon
⅓ cup golden raisins	Salt and freshly ground pepper to taste
3 tablespoons pine nuts	

1. Using a small, sharp knife, make 2 deep slashes in each chicken thigh, one on each side. The slashes should reach the bone.

2. In a large skillet over medium-high heat, melt the butter. Add the chicken thighs and sauté until well browned, about 10 minutes.

3. Add the Cognac and cook until the sauce is reduced to a glaze, about 1 minute. Add the raisins, pine nuts, white wine, Marsala, cinnamon, and salt and pepper, and cook until the sauce thickens somewhat, 5 to 7 minutes. Serve immediately.

Chicken with Green Pea and Mint Sauce

In this lush dish, a velvety green puree supports a moist chicken breast. It is under-

stated elegance.

Preparation time: 20 minutes
Storage: Puree keeps 3 days refrigerated
Serves 4

2 tablespoons butter

4 skinless, boneless
chicken breast halves,
about 6 ounces each

Salt and freshly ground
pepper to taste

1 package (10 ounces)
green peas, thawed

¼ cup heavy cream

6 tablespoons chicken
broth or dry white wine

2 tablespoons
chopped fresh mint

Freshly grated
nutmeg to taste

Fresh mint leaves,
for garnish

1. In a large skillet over medium heat, melt the butter. Add the chicken and cook until browned, 4 to 6 minutes per side. Add the salt and pepper.

2. Meanwhile, prepare the sauce: In a small saucepan over medium-high heat, bring the peas, cream, and broth to a boil. Turn off the heat and stir in the mint, the nutmeg, and salt and pepper to taste.

3. In a food processor or blender, puree the pea mixture until smooth. Pour the sauce onto individual plates and top with the chicken. Garnish with mint sprigs and serve immediately.

Chicken with Watercress, Salsa, and Avocado

Use a fresh, chunky-style salsa for this bright dish.

Preparation time: 15 minutes
Storage: None
Serves 4

2 tablespoons
extra-virgin olive oil

4 skinless, boneless
chicken breast halves,
about 6 ounces each

Salt and freshly ground
pepper to taste

6 cups (2 to 3 bunches)
watercress, cleaned
and stemmed

1 medium avocado, cubed

2 cups chunky salsa,
prepared or homemade
(page 240)

1. In a large skillet over medium heat, heat the olive oil. Add the chicken and cook until browned, 4 to 6 minutes per side. Add the salt and pepper.

2. Place the watercress on a serving platter and put the chicken on top. Sprinkle with the avocado and salsa.

Chicken with Lemon Coriander Vinaigrette

The flavor of this recipe depends on freshly crushed coriander seeds; the ground stuff, unless perfectly fresh, will just not do. This sauce is also wonderful with fish or shrimp, or as a salad dressing.

Preparation time: 15 minutes
Storage: Vinaigrette keeps 3 days refrigerated
Serves 4

8 tablespoons
extra-virgin olive oil

6 skinless, boneless
chicken breast halves,
about 6 ounces each

Salt and freshly ground
pepper to taste

¼ cup lemon juice

1 teaspoon
prepared mustard

½ teaspoon
crushed coriander seeds

1. In a large skillet over medium-high heat, heat 2 tablespoons of the olive oil. Add the chicken and cook until browned, 4 to 6 minutes per side. Add the salt and pepper.

2. Meanwhile, in a small bowl, mix the remaining olive oil, lemon juice, mustard, and coriander. Drizzle over the chicken and serve immediately or at room temperature.

Chicken Sautéed with Artichokes

As always, use the very best marinated artichokes you can find. If you are not sure of a good brand, look for those packed in extra-virgin olive oil.

Preparation time: 15 minutes
Storage: None
Serves 4

¼ cup extra-virgin
olive oil

6 skinless, boneless
chicken breast halves,
about 6 ounces each

Salt and freshly ground
pepper to taste

3 cups sliced marinated
artichoke hearts

2 teaspoons fresh
thyme leaves

2 tablespoons
minced fresh basil

½ cup dry white wine

1. In a large skillet over medium-high heat, heat the olive oil. Add the chicken and cook until browned, 3 to 4 minutes per side. Add the salt and pepper.

2. Stir in the artichoke hearts, thyme, basil, and wine and cook the mixture until the wine evaporates by half, 5 to 6 minutes. Serve immediately.

Variations: Garlic is a welcome addition to this dish.

Turkey Tonnato

I always lighten this traditional veal dish by cutting the sauce with plain yogurt. It is also delicious when served with shrimp, grilled tuna, and of course, veal. If you cannot find imported Italian oil-packed tuna, substitute a domestic oil-packed tuna.

The tonnato sauce is also delicious tossed with tiny boiled red potatoes.

Preparation time: 15 minutes
Storage: Sauce keeps 3 days refrigerated
Serves 6

2 tablespoons
extra-virgin olive oil

6 turkey cutlets,
about 6 ounces each

1 can (6 to 7 ounces)
Italian oil-packed tuna

8 anchovy fillets

¼ cup drained capers
packed in brine,
plus 1 tablespoon
for garnish

1 garlic clove, minced

2 tablespoons
fresh lemon juice

½ cup olive oil

½ cup plain yogurt

Salt and freshly ground
pepper to taste

1. In a large skillet over medium-high heat, heat the olive oil until it is hot but not smoking. Add the turkey and cook until just cooked through, 3 to 5 minutes per side.

2. Meanwhile (or ahead of time) prepare the sauce: In a food processor fitted with a steel blade, process the tuna, anchovies, ¼ cup capers, garlic, lemon juice, olive oil, yogurt, and salt and pepper until smooth.

3. Serve the turkey with the sauce and garnish with more capers, if desired.

Turkey with Walnut and Cilantro Pesto

The sauce for this dish was inspired by the cuisine of Russia, where cilantro and walnuts are commonly combined in a similar type of sauce.

Preparation time: 15 minutes
Storage: Pesto keeps 5 days refrigerated
Serves 6

2 tablespoons
olive oil

6 turkey scaloppini,
about 6 ounces each

Salt and freshly ground
pepper to taste

1 cup toasted walnuts

1 garlic clove

½ cup walnut oil

1 cup cilantro leaves

1. In a large skillet over medium heat, heat the olive oil. Add the turkey and cook until browned, about 3 minutes per side. Add the salt and pepper. Keep warm.

2. Meanwhile, in the food processor or blender, combine the walnuts, garlic, walnut oil, and cilantro and process until smooth. Add salt and pepper to taste. Serve with the turkey.

Turkey with Sun-Dried Tomato and Caper Sauce

The large capers now available in small bottles at specialty stores make a nice garnish for this dish.

Preparation time: 15 minutes
Storage: Sauce keeps 3 days refrigerated
Serves 4

2 tablespoons olive oil	1 cup Sun-Dried Tomato Dip (page 36)
4 turkey scaloppini, about 6 ounces each	1 tablespoon drained capers
Salt and freshly ground pepper to taste	

1. In a large skillet over medium heat, heat the olive oil. Add the turkey and cook until browned, about 3 minutes per side. Add the salt and pepper.

2. Serve the turkey topped with the tomato dip and garnished with the capers.

Turkey Sauté with Chestnuts and Cranberries

This dish is just the thing when you were wondering what to serve for a small Thanksgiving dinner. Use either canned chestnuts or the vacuum-packed variety now available in many markets.

Preparation time: 20 minutes
Storage: None
Serves 4

3 tablespoons butter

6 turkey cutlets,
6 ounces each

Salt and freshly ground
pepper to taste

1 garlic clove, minced

1 shallot, chopped

⅓ cup dry white wine
or chicken broth

2 tablespoons cranberry
sauce, chutney, or relish

½ cup heavy cream

½ pound chestnuts,
roasted and chopped

1. In a large skillet over medium-high heat, melt the butter. Add the turkey and cook until browned, 3 to 4 minutes per side. Add the salt and pepper.

2. Remove the turkey to a platter and keep warm in a 200° F. oven.

3. Add the garlic, shallot, and wine to the pan and raise the heat. Cook until the mixture reduces by half, about 2 minutes. Stir in the cranberry sauce, cream, and chestnuts and cook until the sauce is slightly thickened, about 2 minutes more. Serve immediately over the turkey.

Turkey with Anchovy Butter

This pungent dish has almost too much flavor for the amount of effort put into it. Serve it with buckwheat noodles and green beans, or asparagus in season.

Preparation time: 20 minutes
Storage: Anchovy butter keeps 3 days refrigerated
Serves 4

2 tablespoons
olive oil

4 turkey cutlets,
about 6 ounces each

Salt and freshly ground
pepper to taste

8 anchovy fillets

½ cup (1 stick)
butter, softened

1 tablespoon
fresh tarragon

1. In a large skillet over medium-high heat, heat the olive oil. Add the turkey and cook until browned, 3 to 5 minutes per side. Add the salt and pepper.

2. Meanwhile, in the food processor or blender, combine the anchovies, butter, and tarragon and process until smooth. Slather over the turkey and serve immediately.

meats

Flank Steak with Peanut Sauce and Scallions

Serve this dish with cellophane noodles tossed with more sesame oil and sesame seeds.

Preparation time: 20 minutes
Storage: None
Serves 4

1 flank steak
(about 2 pounds)

3 tablespoons sesame oil

Salt and freshly ground
pepper

6 scallions, trimmed

1 cup peanut sauce,
prepared or homemade
(page 232)

1. Preheat the broiler. Rub the steak with 2 tablespoons of the sesame oil, the salt, and the pepper. Brush the scallions with the remaining sesame oil.

2. Grill the steak for about 5 minutes per side. Add the scallions to the broiler pan when you turn the steak. Let the steak rest for 10 minutes before slicing.

3. Slice the steak diagonally and serve with the peanut sauce and broiled scallions.

Filets Mignon with Red Pepper Butter

Preparation time: 10 minutes

Storage: Red pepper butter keeps 3 days refrigerated

Serves 4

4 filets mignons, about 1½ inches thick	1 tablespoon chopped fresh oregano
½ cup chopped roasted red peppers	Salt and freshly ground pepper
5 tablespoons butter	

1. Preheat the grill or broiler. Grill or broil the steaks for 5 to 7 minutes per side, or to taste.

2. Meanwhile, make the sauce: in a food processor fitted with a steel blade, process the red peppers, butter, oregano, and salt and pepper until smooth. Serve slathered on the steaks.

Variation: Add 1 tablespoon anchovy paste or anchovy fillets to the red pepper butter.

Hanger Steak with Aromatic Carrot Puree

I love the beefy, juicy flavor of a hanger steak, sometimes called butcher's tenderloin or Romanian steak, but if you prefer another cut, use it instead. I owe the inspiration of this dish to Dondi Martin.

Preparation time: 15 minutes
Storage: Carrot puree keeps 3 days refrigerated
Serves 4

Freshly ground pepper

1 tablespoon olive oil

2 hanger steaks,
about 1 inch thick

3 tablespoons butter

1 package (10 ounces)
frozen baby carrots, thawed

1 tablespoon sugar

¼ cup water

¼ teaspoon
garam masala

¼ teaspoon
ground ginger

Freshly grated
nutmeg to taste

Pinch of ground allspice

Salt and freshly ground
pepper to taste

1 tablespoon
heavy cream

1. Preheat the grill or broiler. Rub the pepper and the olive oil on the steaks.

2. Grill or broil the steaks for 2 to 3 minutes per side.

3. Meanwhile, make the sauce: Melt the butter in a large skillet over medium heat. Add the carrots, sugar, and water and cook the mixture until the water evaporates, about 3 minutes. Stir in the garam masala, ginger, nutmeg, allspice, salt and pepper and cook for 1 more minute.

4. Puree the carrot mixture with the cream in a blender or a food processor until it is smooth. Spoon carrot puree onto plates and place the steaks on top. Serve.

Sautéed Boudin Noir with Apples

I eat this dish frequently for brunch, although it is equally good for supper, especially on a chilly Sunday night. I like to serve it with Buttered Spaetzle (page 172) or egg noodles. You can peel the apples if you like, but it's not necessary.

Preparation time: 15 minutes
Storage: None
Serves 2

3 tablespoons butter	3 tablespoons Cognac
6 boudin noir (blood sausage)	Salt and freshly ground pepper to taste
2 small Jonathan or McIntosh apples, cored and sliced	

1. In a large skillet, melt the butter over medium heat. Add the sausage and the apples and sauté for 3 to 5 minutes to brown them.

2. Add the Cognac, salt, and pepper to the pan and lower the heat. Cook until the sausages are done and the apples tender, 5 to 7 more minutes. Serve immediately.

Steak au Poivre with Orange Juice and Apricots

I added orange juice and dried apricots to a classic steak au poivre because I like their sweetness next to the fiery pepper.

Preparation time: 15 minutes
Storage: None
Serves 4

1 cup chicken broth

1 cup orange juice

½ cup chopped
dried apricots

Freshly grated nutmeg

Salt to taste

2 large shell steaks
(also known as New York
strip steaks), about 1 inch
thick, each cut into 2 pieces

4 to 6 teaspoons cracked
black peppercorns

1 tablespoon olive oil

¼ cup Cognac

1. In a small saucepan over high heat, combine the chicken broth, orange juice, and apricots. Cook the mixture until it is reduced by two-thirds, 7 to 10 minutes. Add the nutmeg and salt.

2. Meanwhile, prepare the steaks: Place the steaks on a plate and press the peppercorns into the flesh on both sides. Most of them should adhere to the meat if you press hard.

3. Heat the olive oil in a skillet over medium-high heat and sauté the steaks until they are brown on each side and as done as you like in the center (very rare is 2 to 3 minutes per side).

4. Pour off any remaining fat from the skillet and add the Cognac. Turn the heat off, and carefully ignite the Cognac with a match. The flames will die down quickly.

5. Remove the steaks to a plate and keep warm in a 200° F oven.

6. Add the apricot mixture to the skillet and boil for 1 to 2 minutes, or until the sauce is slightly thickened. Season to taste and pour the sauce over the steaks. Serve immediately.

Veal Chops with Rum and Mint

Use a dry, dark rum such as an anejo for this succulent dish, which I like to serve with yogurt-topped baked sweet potatoes.

Preparation time: 10 minutes
Storage: None
Serves 4

4 tablespoons butter	¼ cup chopped fresh mint
4 veal chops, 1 inch thick	Salt and freshly ground pepper to taste
¼ cup dark rum	

1. In a large skillet, melt 2 tablespoons of the butter over high heat. Add the veal chops and cook for 3 to 5 minutes per side, depending upon how well done you like them.

2. Remove the chops to a platter and keep them warm in a 200° F. oven.

3. Make the sauce: Add the rum to the butter and cook the mixture over high heat, scraping up any browned bits, until it is reduced by one-third. Add the remaining butter, the mint, and the salt and pepper, and serve over the veal.

Veal Cutlets with Prosciutto and Sage

This dish, a simplified version of veal saltimbocca, is delicious served with gnocchi.

Preparation time: 10 minutes
Storage: None
Serves 4

2 tablespoons olive oil	2 tablespoons chopped fresh sage
4 veal cutlets	Salt and freshly ground pepper to taste
3 tablespoons dry white wine	
4 slices prosciutto, slivered	

1. In a large skillet, heat the olive oil over high heat. Add the veal cutlets and cook for about 2 minutes per side, depending upon how well done you like them.

2. Remove the veal cutlets to a platter and keep them warm in a 200° F. oven. Lower the heat to medium.

3. Make the sauce: Add the wine and prosciutto to the pan and cook the mixture, scraping up any browned bits, until the wine reduces slightly, 1 to 2 minutes. Add the sage, and the salt and pepper, and serve over the veal.

Veal Meatballs with Pine Nuts

I like to serve these little morsels unadorned, although they are good dipped in a sauce of half pesto and half yogurt.

Preparation time: 15 minutes
Storage: None
Serves 4

2 garlic cloves	1 pound ground veal
1 very small red onion, quartered	Salt and freshly ground pepper to taste
½ cup fresh basil leaves	1 egg
Pinch of fennel seeds	1 tablespoon olive oil
½ cup pine nuts	2 tablespoons butter

1. In a food processor fitted with a steel blade, process the garlic, onion, and basil until finely chopped. Add the fennel seeds and pine nuts and pulse once or twice to integrate them with the onion mixture. Add the veal, salt, pepper, and egg and pulse to combine. Form the veal mixture into several 2-inch meatballs.

2. Heat the oil and butter in a large skillet over medium-high heat. Add the meatballs and sauté until they are golden brown and crusty on the outside and done to your taste on the inside, 5 to 8 minutes.

3. Serve immediately.

Veal Sautéed in Walnut Oil

Preparation time: 10 minutes

Storage: None

Serves 4

¼ cup walnut oil

4 veal chops,
about 1 inch thick

¾ cup walnuts

Salt and freshly ground
pepper to taste

1 teaspoon
balsamic vinegar

4 tablespoons
chopped chives

1. In a large skillet, heat the oil over high heat. Add the veal chops and the walnuts; cook the chops for 3 to 5 minutes per side, depending upon how well done you like them.

2. Add the salt, pepper, and balsamic vinegar to the pan and cook the mixture, scraping up any browned bits, for 30 seconds. Serve immediately, garnished with the chives.

Variations: Substitute hazelnuts and hazelnut oil for the walnuts and walnut oil.

Grilled Veal Chops with Herbs

Serve this in the summertime with grilled corn and a mesclun salad.

Preparation time: 10 minutes
Storage: None
Serves 4

**4 veal chops,
about ¾ inch thick**

**2 fat garlic cloves,
cut in half**

1 tablespoon olive oil

**2 teaspoons
herbes de Provence**

**Salt and freshly ground
pepper**

1. Preheat the grill or broiler. Rub the veal chops with the garlic, olive oil, herbs, salt, and pepper.

2. Grill the veal for 2 to 3 minutes per side, or to taste.

3. Serve immediately.

Veal Chops with Herbed Goat Cheese Sauce

Use a heady goat cheese, such as Bucheron, for this recipe.

Preparation time: 15 minutes
Storage: Sauce keeps 3 days refrigerated
Serves 4

4 veal chops, about 1 inch thick	2 tablespoons olive oil
⅓ cup heavy cream	2 tablespoons chopped fresh tarragon
1 cup (4 ounces) crumbled goat cheese	Salt and freshly ground pepper to taste
2 garlic cloves, minced	

1. Preheat the grill or broiler. Grill or broil the veal chops for 3 to 4 minutes per side, or to taste.

2. Meanwhile, make the sauce: In a small saucepan over medium heat, bring the cream to a boil. Stir in the goat cheese, garlic, olive oil, tarragon, and salt and pepper. Serve slathered on the chops.

Lamb Chops with Olivada

Preparation time: 10 minutes
Storage: None
Serves 4

Freshly ground pepper	¼ cup olivada, prepared or homemade (page 233)
1 tablespoon olive oil	
4 lamb chops, about 1 inch thick	¼ cup chopped fresh basil leaves

1. Preheat the grill or broiler. Rub the pepper and the olive oil on the lamb chops.

2. Grill or broil the lamb on one side for 3 to 4 minutes. Turn the lamb over and spread the olivada on the uncooked side. Broil the lamb for another 3 to 4 minutes. Serve with the basil.

Lamb Chops with Grainy Mustard-Sherry Butter

If you did not soften the butter in the traditional way (leaving it on the counter for an hour or so), soften it in the microwave. Or don't bother softening the butter and mix the mustard sauce in the food processor.

Preparation time: 10 minutes
Storage: Mustard butter keeps 3 days refrigerated
Serves 4

4 lamb chops, about 1 inch thick	1 tablespoon grainy mustard
2 garlic cloves, cut in half	2 tablespoons dry sherry
1 tablespoon olive oil	1 tablespoon fresh thyme leaves
Salt and freshly ground pepper	
4 tablespoons butter, softened	

1. Preheat the grill or broiler. Rub the lamb chops with the garlic, olive oil, salt, and pepper.

2. Grill the lamb for 3 to 5 minutes per side, or to taste.

3. Meanwhile, make the sauce: In a small bowl, mix the butter, mustard, sherry, and thyme. Serve with the lamb.

Lamb Chops with Sun-Dried Tomatoes and Capers

I like to serve this versatile sauce on chicken and pasta as well as on the lamb chops.

Preparation time: 10 minutes

Storage: Sauce keeps 5 days refrigerated

Serves 4

4 lamb chops,
about 1 inch thick

2 tablespoons
extra-virgin olive oil

⅓ cup oil-packed
sun-dried tomatoes

2 garlic cloves

3 teaspoons drained capers

Salt and freshly ground
pepper to taste

1. Preheat the grill or broiler. Grill or broil the chops for 3 to 5 minutes per side, or to taste.

2. Meanwhile, make the sauce: In a food processor fitted with a steel blade, process the olive oil, sun-dried tomatoes, garlic, capers, and salt and pepper until smooth. Serve slathered on the lamb.

Pork with Dried and Fresh Apples

This classic combination of pork and apples is given new spunk with the addition of dried apples.

Preparation time: 20 minutes
Storage: None
Serves 4

1 tablespoon vegetable oil	1 cup chopped dried apple
1 tablespoon butter	1 cup diced apple
4 pork chops, about 1 inch thick	Salt and freshly ground pepper to taste
3 tablespoons apple cider or white wine	

1. In a large skillet, heat the oil and butter over medium-high heat. Add the pork chops and cook for about 2 minutes per side to brown them.

2. Add the apple cider and dried and fresh apples to the pan and cook the mixture, scraping up any browned bits, for 1 minute. Then cover the pan, reduce the heat to low, and let the mixture simmer until the pork is cooked, about 15 minutes. Add the salt and pepper and serve immediately.

Pork with Pineapple and Lime

This preparation works equally well with chicken or turkey as it does with pork. Just adjust the cooking times accordingly.

Preparation time: 15 minutes
Storage: None
Serves 4

1 tablespoon canola oil	3 tablespoons butter
4 pork tenderloins, about 1 inch thick	Juice of 1 lime
1 cup pineapple juice	Salt and freshly ground pepper to taste
1 tablespoon ginger marmalade	

1. In a large skillet, heat the oil over medium-high heat. Add the pork tenderloins and brown them on both sides, about 2 minutes.

2. Add the pineapple juice and marmalade and cook until the pork is just cooked through and the sauce reduced by about half, 7 to 10 minutes. Add the butter, lime juice, salt, and pepper and sauté for 1 minute more. Serve immediately.

Variations: If you can't find ginger marmalade, substitute lime marmalade and add ginger (1 tablespoon grated fresh ginger or $\frac{1}{2}$ teaspoon ground).

fish and other seafood

Poached Bay Scallops in Ginger-Beet Broth

Using vegetable juices as light sauces and broths was the brilliant creation of Jean-Georges Vongerichten, the chef at JoJo and Vong in New York City. However, Vongerichten's recipes generally include several time-consuming and messy steps requiring a juice extractor.

Luckily for those of us with less time, we can buy fresh vegetable juices at most health food stores with juice bars or in bottles. Biotta, from Switzerland, is an excellent brand, made with organic vegetables (see Sources, page vi).

The combination of sweet, magenta beet juice and pure-white briny scallops is wonderful. However, the beet juice reduction can also be used with fish, such as black bass (which is how Jean-Georges serves it), shrimp, or grilled tuna steaks. It might even work well with beefsteak, although I have never tried it. Let your imagination fly.

In this recipe I have used tiny bay scallops, but if you can find only sea scallops, quarter them before poaching.

Preparation time: 15–20 minutes
Storage: Reduced beet juice keeps 3 days refrigerated
Serves 4

1 quart beet juice	2 tablespoons butter
3½-inch-thick slices fresh ginger	Salt and freshly ground pepper to taste
1½ pounds bay scallops	Chopped fresh chives

1. In a large saucepan, combine the beet juice and the ginger. Bring the mixture to a boil over medium heat, then raise the heat to high and boil the mixture until it reduces by half, 10 to 15 minutes.

2. While the beet juice is reducing, place just enough water in a large saucepan to cover the scallops. Bring the water to a boil. Place the scallops in the boiling water and lower the heat. Simmer the scallops for about 1 minute, then immediately drain them and reserve. Do not overcook the scallops or they will be rubbery.

3. When the beet juice is reduced, pick out the ginger with a slotted spoon. Then whisk in the butter and stir until the sauce thickens a bit. Remove from the heat and stir in the salt and pepper.

4. Divide the scallops among 4 soup plates. Spoon some of the beet juice around them. Grind on more fresh pepper and garnish with the chives. Serve immediately.

Sea Scallops with Salmon Caviar

This is the perfect party entree because it is both sumptuous and simple. The same sauce can be served with roasted or sautéed salmon fillets.

Preparation time: 10 minutes
Storage: None
Serves 4

¾ cups crème fraîche or heavy cream	2 pounds sea scallops
2 tablespoons Cognac	Freshly ground pepper to taste
1 tablespoon lemon zest	Chive strands
¼ cup (about 2 ounces) salmon caviar	

1. In a small saucepan, bring the crème fraîche and the Cognac to a boil over high heat. Boil the mixture until it reduces and thickens, about 3 minutes. Remove pan from heat and stir in the lemon zest and all but 1 heaping tablespoon of caviar.

2. Meanwhile, place just enough water in a large saucepan to cover the scallops. Bring the water to a boil. Place the scallops in the boiling water and lower the heat. Simmer the scallops for about 1 minute, then immediately drain them and reserve. Do not overcook the scallops or they will be rubbery.

3. Divide the scallops among 4 plates. Spoon the sauce over the scallops and grind on the pepper. Sprinkle the remaining caviar over the scallops, then top with the chives. Serve immediately.

Shrimp in Spicy Carrot Juice

This is yet another dish inspired by Jean-Georges Vongerichten's Simple Cuisine. At JoJo, Vongerichten serves this dish as an appetizer, but I think it makes a splendid entree, especially when paired with Polenta (page 242).

You have two options to obtain carrot juice: you could juice ten carrots in a juicer if you have a juicer and the time, or you could go to your local health food store and buy either freshly squeezed carrot juice or bottled carrot juice.

Preparation time: 10 minutes
Storage: None
Serves 4

2 cups carrot juice	3 tablespoons butter
Pinch of freshly ground nutmeg	Salt and cayenne pepper to taste
Pinch of ground cinnamon	2 pounds large shrimp, cleaned
Pinch of ground cardamom	Chopped chervil or chives
1 teaspoon fresh lemon juice	

1. In a medium saucepan over medium heat, combine the carrot juice, spices, and lemon juice. Slowly whisk in 2 tablespoons of the butter, until the sauce thickens somewhat. Bring the sauce to a boil, then remove from the heat and add the salt and cayenne pepper.

2. In a large skillet, melt the remaining 1 tablespoon of butter. When the foam begins to subside, add the shrimp and sauté until the shrimp just begin to turn pink, 1 to 2 minutes. Immediately remove the pan from the heat and keep the shrimp warm.

3. To serve, place about 8 shrimp in each of 4 soup plates. Spoon the carrot juice over the top. Garnish with the chervil.

Chile-Lime Shrimp Brochettes

This incredibly easy dish just explodes with flavor. Serve it over fresh pasta or with Couscous Salad with Chickpeas, Orange, and Mint (page 62).

Don't forget to wear rubber gloves when handling the chiles.

Preparation time: 15 minutes, plus marinating
Storage: Shrimp marinate overnight, refrigerated
Serves 4

¼ cup extra-virgin olive oil	2 tablespoons chopped cilantro
2 tablespoons lime juice	2 pounds large shrimp, cleaned
1 jalapeño chile, seeded and minced	Salt to taste

1. In a large bowl, combine the olive oil, lime juice, jalapeño, salt, and cilantro, mixing well. Add the shrimp, tossing to coat them with the marinade. Let the mixture marinate for 30 to 45 minutes at room temperature, or for several hours in the refrigerator, stirring occasionally.

2. Preheat broiler. Thread the shrimp onto 4 bamboo skewers. Broil the shrimp until they just turn pink, about 1 minute per side. Serve immediately.

Salsa Scallops with Avocado

Preparation time: 10 minutes
Storage: None
Serves 4

2 tablespoons
olive oil

2 pounds
sea scallops

Salt and freshly ground
pepper to taste

¾ cup salsa,
prepared or homemade
(page 240)

1 avocado, peeled,
pitted, and sliced

1. In a large skillet, heat 1 tablespoon of the olive oil until it is hot but not smoking. Add as many scallops as comfortably fit into the pan in one layer. Sear the scallops on both sides, then remove them from the pan and keep warm. Continue to sear the scallops in batches, adding more oil if necessary, until all of them are cooked.

2. Divide the scallops among 4 plates and sprinkle on the salt and pepper. Spoon some of the salsa around them, and top with the avocado. Serve immediately.

Ale-Poached Shrimp with Honey Mustard Sauce

This is a perfect picnic dish because the shrimp can be poached in advance, and there is something about peel-and-eat shrimp that makes me want to eat them outdoors.

Preparation time: 15 minutes
Storage: Poached shrimp keep 24 hours refrigerated
Serves 4–6

2 bottles (12 ounces each) ale or beer

1 teaspoon dried thyme

3 bay leaves

8 garlic cloves, smashed

1 teaspoon caraway seeds

Dash of Tabasco

1 cup honey mustard

1 cup sour cream or plain yogurt

2 pounds unpeeled shrimp

1. In a large saucepan, bring the ale, thyme, bay leaves, garlic, caraway seeds, and Tabasco to a boil over high heat. Reduce the heat to medium and simmer the mixture for 10 minutes.

2. Meanwhile, prepare the mustard sauce: In a small bowl, combine the mustard and sour cream, stirring well.

3. Add the shrimp to the beer broth and simmer until they just turn pink, about 1 minute. Immediately drain the shrimp and serve hot or at room temperature, with the mustard sauce on the side.

Shrimp with Balsamic Vinegar

For a colorful hors d'oeuvre, marinate the shrimp with a cup of red and/or yellow cherry tomatoes and a cup of steamed broccoli florets, and present them on skewers. For a first course, serve the shrimp nestled inside purple radicchio leaves and topped with shredded basil leaves. And as an entree, spoon the shrimp over basic Grilled Polenta (page 242), or surround a tower of Green Bean Salad with Walnuts and Pecorino (page 65) with these flavorful gems.

Preparation time: 5 minutes, plus 30 minutes standing
Storage: 24 hours, refrigerated
Serves 4 as an entree, 6–8 as a first course

2 tablespoons olive oil	2 cups Balsamic Vinaigrette (page 235)
2 pounds shrimp, cleaned	

1. In a large skillet over high heat, heat the olive oil until hot but not smoking. Add the shrimp and sauté until they just begin to turn pink, 1 to 2 minutes. Immediately remove shrimp from heat.

2. In a large bowl, combine the warm shrimp and the vinaigrette. Let the mixture marinate at room temperature for 30 minutes to 1 hour. Serve immediately. Alternatively, you may marinate the shrimp in the refrigerator for up to 24 hours. Let the shrimp come to room temperature before serving (take them out of the refrigerator at least 1 hour before serving).

Hazelnut Shrimp with Endive

Since I serve these wonderfully nutty shrimp as an hors d'oeuvre at almost every cocktail party I give, I am always amazed that none of my friends are tired of them. Although I have made them directly before serving, they are even better if they have been allowed to sit at room temperature for thirty minutes or so.

Preparation time: 10 minutes
Storage: 2 days, refrigerated
Serves 6–10 as an hors d'oeuvre

1 pound shrimp, cleaned	**Freshly grated nutmeg to taste**
6 tablespoons hazelnut oil	**Salt and freshly ground pepper to taste**
2 tablespoons lemon juice	**2 to 3 endives, leaves separated**
¼ cup chopped toasted hazelnuts	

1. In a large saucepan, bring enough water to cover the shrimp to a boil over high heat. Lower the heat to medium and add the shrimp. Cook until they just turn pink, about 1 minute. Drain and reserve.

2. In a large bowl, combine the hazelnut oil, lemon juice, hazelnuts, nutmeg, and salt and pepper. Add the warm shrimp, tossing to distribute the dressing. If possible, let the mixture stand at room temperature for 20 to 45 minutes.

3. When ready to serve, spoon some of the shrimp mixture into the endive leaves. Serve immediately.

Soy-Roasted Tuna Steaks

The meatiness of tuna holds up well to a salty soy-sauce marinade.

If you can find lemon tamari, you can use it in place of the lemon juice and soy sauce; it will give your fish a slightly caramelized flavor.

Preparation time: 25–40 minutes, included marinating
Storage: Fish marinates several hours, refrigerated
Serves 4

½ cup soy sauce

2 tablespoons
lemon juice

2 tablespoons chili,
sesame, or olive oil,
or a combination

2 garlic cloves, chopped,
or 2 teaspoons prepared
minced garlic

4 small tuna steaks,
1 inch thick, about 6
ounces each

1. In a large, flat dish, combine the soy sauce, lemon juice, oil, and garlic, mixing well. Place the tuna steaks in the marinade, turning to coat them. Let marinate for 15 to 30 minutes at room temperature or several hours in the refrigerator.

2. Preheat the oven to 450° F. Transfer tuna to an oiled baking sheet, shaking off extraneous garlic pieces. Roast the tuna steaks until done to your taste, 8 to 10 minutes, turning them once. Serve immediately.

Broiled Tuna Steaks with Red Pepper Sauce and Capers

An extremely easy, impressive dish.

Preparation time: 15 minutes
Storage: Red pepper sauce keeps 3 days refrigerated
Serves 4

½ cup roasted red peppers,
rinsed if necessary

¼ cup heavy cream
or yogurt

2 teaspoons fresh thyme
or ½ teaspoon dried

Salt and freshly ground
pepper to taste

4 small tuna steaks,
1 inch thick, about 6
ounces each

2 tablespoons olive oil

2 tablespoons drained capers

1. In a food processor or blender, process the red peppers, cream, and thyme until very smooth. Taste and add the salt and pepper.

2. Preheat the broiler. Oil a baking sheet and arrange the tuna on top. Brush with the olive oil. Broil the fish until it is done to your taste, 6 to 10 minutes.

3. To serve, place a tuna steak on each of 4 plates. Spoon some of the red pepper sauce around the tuna. Garnish with the capers.

Tuna in White Bean Broth with Sage

A very light entree that needs no further embellishment other than good sourdough bread to sop up the white bean broth.

Preparation time: 15 minutes
Storage: None
Serves 4

4 small tuna steaks,
1 inch thick, about
6 ounces each

2 tablespoons
olive oil

Salt and freshly ground
pepper to taste

1 recipe White Bean
Broth with Sage
(page 42)

Sprigs of fresh sage,
for garnish

1. Preheat the broiler. Oil a baking sheet. Arrange the tuna on the baking sheet, brush with the olive oil, and season with the salt and pepper.

2. Broil the fish for 6 to 10 minutes, or to taste.

3. While the fish is broiling, heat the white bean broth to a simmer, stirring constantly, in a large saucepan. Remove from the heat.

4. To serve, place a tuna steak in each of 4 soup plates. Top with the white bean broth. Garnish with the fresh sage.

Roasted Salmon with Bay Leaf–Orange Butter and Cashews

The woodsy bay leaf and sweet orange combination really sets this simple, zesty dish apart.

Preparation time: 15 minutes
Storage: Sauce keeps 2 days refrigerated
Serves 4

1 tablespoon olive oil

4 salmon fillets, about 6 ounces each

6 tablespoons butter

3 bay leaves

¼ cup chopped cashews

3 tablespoons orange juice, fresh if possible

1 tablespoon grated orange zest (optional)

2 tablespoons chopped fresh parsley

Salt and freshly ground pepper to taste

1. Preheat oven to 450° F. Oil a baking sheet with some of the olive oil. Arrange the salmon fillets on the baking sheet and brush them with the remaining oil. Roast the salmon until it is done to your taste, 8 to 13 minutes.

2. Meanwhile, prepare the sauce: In a small saucepan, melt the butter. Add the bay leaves and cashews and cook until the nuts are toasted, about 3 minutes. Stir in the remaining ingredients and cook for 2 minutes longer. Remove the bay leaves and serve immediately, spooning the sauce over the salmon.

Pistachioed Red Snapper

A crunchy crust of pistachio nuts gives way to the melting, sweet flesh of red snapper in this easy preparation. Team it with Middle Eastern Carrot Salad (page 55) for an unusual combination.

Feel free to substitute other firm-fleshed white fish such as flounder or sea bass for the snapper.

Preparation time: 20 minutes
Storage: None
Serves 4

¾ cup finely chopped pistachio nuts

4 skinless red snapper fillets, about 6 ounces each

2 tablespoons orange juice

Salt and freshly ground pepper to taste

2 tablespoons butter

1 tablespoon olive oil

1. Lay the pistachio nuts in a flat dish. Brush each snapper fillet on both sides with the orange juice. Season the fish well with the salt and pepper. Dredge the fish on both sides in the pistachios, pressing the nuts into the fillets with your hands so they form a thick crust.

2. In a large skillet over medium-high heat, melt 1 tablespoon butter with ½ tablespoon olive oil. When the foam from the butter has subsided, add 2 of the fish fillets. Sauté the fish for 2 to 3 minutes per side, or until it is just done. Remove the fish from the pan and keep warm. Sauté the remaining fillets in the remaining butter and olive oil. Serve the fish immediately.

Red Snapper with Creamy Pesto

This dish is perfect to serve with steamed tiny red potatoes, which can be dipped into the pesto. Make sure to use a good brand of pesto for this.

You can substitute flounder or halibut for the snapper.

Preparation time: 15 minutes
Storage: None
Serves 4

½ cup pesto sauce, prepared or homemade (page 234)

½ cup sour cream or yogurt

Salt and freshly ground pepper to taste

4 red snapper fillets, about 6 ounces each

Juice of ½ lemon

Lemon wedges, for garnish

1. Preheat the broiler.

2. In a small bowl, combine the pesto and sour cream, mixing well. Taste and add the salt and pepper.

3. Oil a baking sheet and arrange the snapper fillets on the sheet. Squeeze the lemon juice over them and broil for 6 to 8 minutes, depending on the thickness of the fish (the rule is about 10 minutes per inch, measured at the thickest part of the fish).

4. To serve, place a snapper fillet on each of 4 plates, spoon some of the pesto around it, and garnish with the lemon wedges.

Swordfish with Olivada and Potato "Scales"

In this dish, thin slices of cooked potatoes are laid over olivada-encrusted swordfish steaks. The fish is then quickly broiled, so the potatoes get slightly crunchy and the fish remains moist. Serve this dish with a simple watercress salad on the side.

Olivada is easily found in many large supermarkets, and although San Remo makes my favorite version, many excellent ones are available.

Preparation time: 20 minutes
Storage: Boiled potatoes keep 4 days refrigerated
Serves 4

½ cup black olivada, prepared or homemade (page 233)	4 small swordfish steaks, 1 inch thick, about 6 ounces each
¼ cup chopped fresh basil or parsley	2 potatoes, cooked, peeled, and thinly sliced
1 tablespoon lemon juice (optional)	2 tablespoons olive oil

1. Preheat the broiler.

2. In a small bowl, combine the olivada, basil, and lemon juice.

3. Oil a baking sheet and arrange the swordfish steaks on the sheet. Spread with the olivada mixture and top with overlapping potato slices. Brush with olive oil.

4. Broil the fish until the potatoes are browned and the fish cooked, 8 to 10 minutes. Serve immediately.

Margarita Swordfish

You can substitute tuna or tilefish for the swordfish.

Preparation time: 20 minutes, plus marinating
Storage: Fish marinates overnight, refrigerated
Serves 4

3 limes

¼ cup tequila

3 tablespoons
chopped fresh cilantro

¼ cup olive oil

4 small swordfish steaks,
1 inch thick, about
6 ounces each

Salt and freshly ground
pepper to taste

Lime wedges,
for garnish

Cilantro sprigs,
for garnish

1. Grate the zest from 1 of the limes into a small bowl. Then juice all 3 into the same bowl. Stir in the tequila, chopped cilantro, and olive oil.

2. Arrange the swordfish in 1 layer in a large, shallow dish. Pour the lime juice mixture over the fish, turning to coat. Marinate the fish for 30 minutes to 1 hour at room temperature or for several hours in the refrigerator.

3. Preheat the broiler. Oil a baking pan. Place the fish on the prepared pan, shaking off any excess marinade. Grind on the salt and pepper. Broil, turning the steaks once, until the fish is just cooked through, 8 to 10 minutes. Serve immediately, with the lime wedges and cilantro for garnish.

Seafood Stew in a Spiced Citrus Broth

Although this recipe looks complicated because of the long ingredient list, using ready-cleaned vegetables from the salad bar in your supermarket makes it a snap to prepare. And it is all done in twenty minutes.

Serve this stew over rice or alone, accompanied by crisp baguettes. It is perfect for feeding a crowd.

Preparation time: 20 minutes
Storage: Broth keeps 1 day refrigerated
Serves 4–6

½ cup diced carrot	¼ teaspoon anise seeds
1 kirby cucumber, peeled and diced	1 pound shrimp, cleaned
½ cup diced mushrooms	1 pound scallops
1 cup dry white wine	Salt and freshly ground pepper to taste
1 cup freshly squeezed orange juice	3 tablespoons chopped fresh basil or parsley
2 tablespoons lime juice	
1 tablespoon freshly grated ginger	

1. In a large saucepan, combine the vegetables, wine, orange juice, lime juice, ginger, and anise. Bring the mixture to a boil over high heat, then lower the heat and simmer the mixture for 15 minutes.

2. Add the shrimp and scallops and simmer for 1 minute more. Add the salt, pepper, and herbs and serve immediately.

Herbed Salmon Tartare

This colorful dish makes a terrific do-ahead hors d'oeuvre or first course. Serve small scoops on top of radish slices or buttered slices of dark pumpernickel bread as a pass-around cocktail nibble; or serve larger scoops over mixed baby lettuces, with crisp toast and butter on the side. Use only very fresh salmon for this dish, since it is eaten raw.

Preparation time: 10 minutes, plus 20 minutes chilling
Storage: Several hours refrigerated
Serves 4 as a first course, 8–10 as an hors d'oeuvre

1 pound skinless
salmon fillets

¼ cup fresh lemon juice

3 tablespoons finely
chopped red onion

1 tablespoon
extra-virgin olive oil

1 tablespoon fresh
chopped chervil or
thyme leaves

Freshly ground
pepper to taste

½ cup chopped
basil, for rolling

1. Using either a food processor fitted with a metal blade or a knife, chop the salmon very fine. If using a food processor, be careful not to overprocess and puree the fish.

2. Place the salmon in a large bowl. Add the lemon juice, onion, olive oil, chervil, and pepper, and mix well to combine. Refrigerate mixture for at least 20 minutes to allow the flavors to blend.

3. When ready to serve, shape the tartare into balls and roll them in the chopped basil to coat.

Squid Salad with Herbs

This makes a lovely first course, or serve it as a light entree.

Preparation time: 15 minutes
Storage: 3 days refrigerated
Serves 6

¼ cup olive oil

2 pounds cleaned
squid, sliced into ½-inch rings

1 tablespoon lemon juice

2 tablespoons orange juice

2 garlic cloves,
minced, or 2 teaspoons
prepared minced garlic

2 tablespoons
chopped fresh mint

2 tablespoons
chopped fresh basil

2 cups chopped tomato
(2–3 large tomatoes)

Salt and freshly ground
pepper to taste

1. In a large skillet, heat 1 tablespoon of the olive oil until it is hot but not smoking. Add the squid to the pan and sauté until the squid just turns opaque, 1 to 2 minutes. Immediately remove from heat. Do not overcook the squid or it will be rubbery.

2. In a large bowl, combine all the ingredients, tossing to coat the squid in the dressing. Taste and correct the seasonings.

Spicy Crab Cakes with Vinegared Oranges

You may also fry up miniature crab cakes and serve them, without the sauce, with cocktails.

Preparation time: 15 minutes
Storage: crab patties keep 6 hours refrigerated
Serves 4 as an entree, 6–8 as an appetizer

1 pound lump
crab meat

2 large eggs,
lightly beaten

½ cup chopped
red onion (optional)

2 tablespoons
drained capers

⅛ teaspoon
cayenne pepper

3 tablespoons
chopped fresh chives
or parsley

1½ cups cracker crumbs
or fresh bread crumbs

Salt to taste

3 tablespoons
olive oil

Vinegared Oranges (optional)
(recipe follows)

1. In a large bowl, combine the crab meat, eggs, onion, capers, cayenne pepper, chives or parsley, 1 cup of the cracker crumbs, and the salt. Mix well.

2. Form the crab mixture into patties and dredge them in the remaining cracker crumbs. (If you are making the crab cakes ahead, wrap tightly and refrigerate.)

3. Heat half the olive oil in a large skillet. Fry the crab cakes in batches, adding more olive oil as necessary, until they are golden brown, about 2 minutes per side. Drain them on paper towels and serve immediately—with the vinegared oranges, if desired.

Vinegared Oranges

Preparation time: 10 minutes
Storage: Sauce keeps 6 hours refrigerated
Makes 1½ cups

2 seedless oranges	½ teaspoon honey
2 tablespoons balsamic vinegar	Freshly ground pepper to taste

1. Peel the oranges and divide them into sections.

2. In a small saucepan, combine the balsamic vinegar and the honey. Heat the mixture over medium heat, stirring, until the honey melts. Remove pan from heat.

3. Add the oranges and pepper, stirring to combine. Serve with the crab cakes.

vegetables and side dishes

Buttered Spaetzle

These small egg dumplings are an elegant way to replace buttered noodles. Serve them wherever there is a savory sauce waiting to be sopped up. This recipe may seem too easy to be in a cookbook, but I want to remind you about spaetzle in case you forget.

Preparation time: 20 minutes
Storage: 2 days refrigerated
Serves 4–6

1 box (15 ounces) spaetzle	**Salt and freshly ground pepper to taste**
3 tablespoons butter	

1. Cook the spaetzle according to the package directions.

2. Drain and toss with the butter, salt, and pepper.

Variations: Add up to $1/2$ cup grated Gruyère or Parmesan cheese to this dish. Just stir it into the hot spaetzle, which will melt the cheese beautifully. Chopped fresh herbs are also nice.

Cumin Couscous with Zucchini

I like to use whole-wheat couscous for this aromatic side dish, which can be served hot or cold.

Preparation time: 20 minutes
Storage: 2 days refrigerated
Serves 4–6

1 cup couscous, regular or whole-wheat	**2 plum tomatoes, diced**
2 small zucchini, sliced	**Fresh lemon juice to taste (optional)**
1¼ cups boiling chicken broth or water	**Salt and freshly ground pepper**
2 tablespoons olive oil	
1 teaspoon cumin seeds	

1. In a large bowl, combine the couscous, zucchini, and boiling broth. Cover the bowl with a dish towel and let it stand until the couscous has absorbed all the water, about 12 minutes. Fluff the mixture with a fork.

2. In a small skillet over medium heat, heat the olive oil until it is hot but not smoking. Add the cumin seeds and cook until they release their scent, about 30 seconds. Turn off the heat.

3. Stir the cumin oil and tomatoes into the couscous mixture. Taste and add the lemon juice if desired, and the salt and pepper. Either serve immediately or store.

Variations: Chopped fresh cilantro or fresh basil, up to ¼ cup, is very nice in this dish.

Bulgur Pilaf with Dried Cranberries and Pecans

There are several different sizes of bulgur available on the market. Use a medium grain if you have a choice.

Preparation time: 15 minutes, plus steeping
Storage: 2 days refrigerated
Serves 4–6

1 cup bulgur

½ cup dried cranberries

2 cups chicken broth

2 tablespoons
butter or olive oil

1 large yellow onion,
coarsely chopped

½ cup pecan halves

2 garlic cloves, minced

Salt and freshly ground
pepper to taste

1. In a medium saucepan, bring the bulgur, cranberries, and chicken broth to a boil. Remove from the heat and let the mixture sit, covered, for 30 minutes. Fluff the bulgur with a fork.

2. In a large skillet, heat the butter or olive oil, then add the onion and sauté over medium-low heat until the onion is translucent and soft, about 5 minutes. Add the pecans and sauté for another 3 minutes, until the pecans release their fragrance and begin to turn golden. Add the garlic and sauté until the garlic turns opaque but does not brown, 1 minute more.

3. Add the bulgur mixture to the skillet and mix it well with the onion and pecans. Remove from the heat. Taste and correct seasonings. Serve immediately.

Variations: For a bit of color, substitute 3 trimmed and sliced scallions for the onion.

Pink Mashed Potatoes

Potatoes cook amazingly quickly in the microwave, and since they bake and not boil, they make the most delicious mashed potatoes imaginable. In this savory recipe, pinto beans add a subtle flavor and lovely color. Use whatever herbs you have on hand. Basil and chervil are especially nice.

Preparation time: 15 minutes, plus steeping
Storage: 2 days refrigerated
Serves 4–6

3 baking potatoes, scrubbed

1 can (16 ounces) pinto beans, rinsed

2 garlic cloves, minced

3 tablespoons chopped fresh herbs

Juice of ½ lemon

1 tablespoon red wine vinegar

2 tablespoons extra-virgin olive oil, preferably flavored

Salt and freshly ground pepper to taste

1. Prick the potatoes all over with a fork. Place them on a microwave-safe plate and microwave them on high power for about 16 minutes. You can peel the potatoes, if you desire, although I never do.

2. Using a food processor, an electric mixer, or a fork, mash the potatoes with the beans, garlic, herbs, lemon juice, vinegar, olive oil, and salt and pepper. Serve immediately.

Red Pepper Mousse

This silky side dish also works well when served as an hors d'oeuvre. Simply scoop some of the mousse into endive leaves and display them on a large, round platter.

Preparation time: 15 minutes, plus chilling
Storage: 2 days refrigerated
Serves 2

3 roasted red peppers

⅓ cup plain yogurt

Salt and freshly ground pepper

1 packet powdered unflavored gelatin

1. Process the peppers, yogurt, and seasonings in the food processor until perfectly smooth.

2. Heat ¼ cup of the mixture over low heat until it is hot to the touch. Sprinkle in the gelatin and stir to dissolve it. Stir in the remaining pepper mixture.

3. Pour the mixture into 2 small ramekins and refrigerate until set, 2 to 3 hours.

Variations: Add 2 tablespoons chopped fresh herbs, especially basil or chives, and/or 1 minced garlic clove, and/or 1 teaspoon chopped shallots softened in butter, and/or 1 teaspoon balsamic vinegar.

Pan-Fried Artichokes

This dish is one of my favorites. Artichokes bathed with wine and garlic—what could be better?

Preparation time: 15 minutes
Storage: 2 days refrigerated
Serves 4

3 tablespoons
olive oil

2 packages (10 ounces each)
frozen quartered artichoke
hearts, thawed

5 garlic cloves, minced

1 cup dry white wine

2 tablespoons
lemon juice

Salt and freshly ground
pepper to taste

¼ cup finely chopped
fresh basil or parsley

1. Heat the olive oil in a large, preferably nonstick skillet until it is hot but not smoking.

2. Add the artichokes and garlic and sauté until the garlic turns opaque, about 1 minute. Add the wine and lemon juice and simmer the mixture until most of the liquid has evaporated. Season with salt and pepper to taste and serve either hot or at room temperature, garnished with the herbs.

Green Beans with Sesame and Soy

This wonderfully flavorful dish can be served warm or at room temperature as a side dish, or chilled and served as a salad. Garnish it with sesame seeds, if you have them on hand.

Preparation time: 10-15 minutes
Storage: 2 days refrigerated
Serves 4–6

1 pound green
beans, trimmed

2 garlic cloves, minced

3 tablespoons
olive oil

1 tablespoon
soy sauce

1 tablespoon
Asian sesame oil

Pinch of hot
red pepper flakes

Salt to taste

1. Bring a large pot of water to a boil. Add the green beans and cook until they are done to your taste. (I cook them for about 2 minutes total.) Drain and refresh under cold water. Alternatively, cook the green beans in the microwave by rinsing them in water, then placing the wet beans in a microwavable plastic bag. Cook them at high power for about 7 minutes or to taste.

2. While the beans are cooking, make the dressing: In a small bowl, mix the garlic, olive oil, soy sauce, sesame oil, pepper flakes, and salt.

3. Place the green beans in a large serving bowl. Pour on the dressing and toss to combine.

Sautéed Cucumbers with Tarragon

European, or hothouse, cucumbers are the long cellophane-wrapped variety that do not need to be peeled or seeded. If you cannot find them, you will need to peel and seed the regular kind.

Preparation time: 10 minutes
Storage: None
Serves 2–4

2 tablespoons butter

1 seedless European
cucumber, thinly sliced

Salt and freshly ground
pepper

1 tablespoon chopped
fresh tarragon leaves

1. In a large pan over medium-high heat, melt the butter. When the foam subsides, add the cucumber and sauté until it wilts, 2 to 4 minutes.

2. Add the salt, pepper, and tarragon and serve immediately.

Variations: If you want to gild the lily, add 2 to 4 tablespoons of heavy cream or crème fraîche to this dish with the cucumbers.

Sautéed Fennel with Pernod

Be sure to save the feathery green tops to the fennel bulbs. They make a spectacular garnish.

Preparation time: 15 minutes
Storage: 2 days refrigerated
Serves 4–6

3 tablespoons olive oil	2 tablespoons Pernod
4 small fennel bulbs, trimmed (tops reserved)	Salt and freshly ground pepper to taste

1. In a large pan over medium heat, heat the olive oil until it is hot but not smoking. Add the fennel and Pernod and cover the pan. Cook the mixture until the fennel wilts, 7 to 10 minutes, checking every 2 minutes to see if the mixture looks on the verge of browning. If so, add a few tablespoons of water to the pan.

2. When the fennel is soft, add the salt and pepper and serve immediately, garnished with the fennel tops.

Cauliflower with Anchovies

Cutting up the cauliflower is the most time-consuming thing about this easy recipe. If you want to cook the cauliflower in the microwave instead of steaming it, you might save another minute or two, and you won't have the pot to wash.

Preparation time: 15 minutes
Storage: 2 days refrigerated
Serves 4–6

1 head cauliflower, cut into florets	2 tablespoons red wine vinegar
4 anchovy fillets	Salt and freshly ground pepper to taste
2 garlic cloves	
½ cup extra-virgin olive oil	

1. Place about 1 inch of water on the bottom of a large pot with a tight-fitting lid. Place the steamer basket in the pot and turn the heat to high. When the water is boiling, add the cauliflower florets, cover the pot, and cook until the florets are done to your taste. (I cook them for about 6 minutes.) Remove the steamer basket from the pot. Alternatively, cook the cauliflower florets in the microwave by rinsing them in water, then placing the wet florets in a microwavable plastic bag. Cook them at high power for 6 or so minutes, or to taste.

2. While the cauliflower is cooking, make the dressing: In a food processor or blender, combine the anchovies and garlic and process until they are finely chopped. Add the olive oil, vinegar, and salt and pepper and pulse to combine.

3. Place the cauliflower in a large serving bowl. Pour on the dressing and toss to combine. The warm cauliflower will greedily absorb the dressing.

White Beans with Red Onions

Preparation time: 10 minutes

Storage: 3 days refrigerated

Serves 2–4

1 can (16 ounces)
white beans, rinsed

1 garlic clove,
minced

2 tablespoons
olive oil

1 tablespoon fresh
lemon or lime juice

Salt and freshly ground
pepper to taste

1 small red onion, sliced

1. In a medium bowl, combine the beans, garlic, olive oil, lemon juice, and salt and pepper. Mix well.

2. Spread the bean mixture on a serving platter. Top with the onion.

Variation: To turn this side dish into a light meal, add 1 can of tuna, preferably Italian oil-packed, to the salad just before serving. Chopped fresh Italian parsley makes a nice garnish.

Ginger Glazed Carrots

If you can find Wilkin and Sons (Tiptree) ginger fruit spread, use it in this recipe. Otherwise, regular ginger marmalade works just fine.

Preparation time: 10 minutes
Storage: 2 days refrigerated
Serves 4

2 tablespoons butter

1 package
(10 ounces) frozen
baby carrots, thawed

2 tablespoons
orange juice or water

1 tablespoon
ginger fruit spread or
marmalade

½ teaspoon
ground ginger

Salt and freshly ground
pepper to taste

1. In a large pan over medium-high heat, melt the butter. When the foam subsides, add the carrots and orange juice and sauté until the liquid evaporates, about 2 minutes.

2. Stir in the marmalade, ginger, salt, and pepper and cook for 1 minute more. Serve immediately.

Variations: Substitute orange marmalade for the ginger.

Instant Succotash

The addition of fresh herbs revitalizes the frozen vegetables.

Preparation time: 10 minutes
Storage: 2 days refrigerated
Serves 4–6

2 tablespoons
olive oil

2 garlic cloves

1 package
frozen corn kernels

1 package frozen
baby lima beans

3 tablespoons
chopped fresh basil
or parsley

¼ cup heavy cream

1 tablespoon
chopped fresh
oregano or chives

Salt and freshly ground
pepper to taste

1. In a large pan over medium-high heat, heat the olive oil until it is hot but not smoking. Add the garlic, corn, and lima beans and sauté until the vegetables are defrosted and the liquid evaporates, about 4 minutes. Add the cream, reduce for 2 minutes, and add the herbs.

2. Stir in the salt and pepper and serve immediately.

Variation: If you prefer, leave out the cream. For an added bite, sauté ½ to 1 jalapeño chile with the garlic.

Sautéed Zucchini

Use half green zucchini and half yellow summer squash for a vivid color contrast.

Preparation time: 10 minutes
Storage: None
Serves 2–4

2 tablespoons
olive oil

2 garlic cloves

4 small zucchini,
sliced

¼ cup freshly grated
Parmesan cheese

2 tablespoons
minced fresh basil

Salt and freshly ground
pepper to taste

1. In a large pan heat the olive oil over medium-high heat until it is hot but not smoking. Add the garlic and zucchini and sauté until the zucchini is wilted, about 4 minutes.

2. Stir in the Parmesan cheese, basil, salt, and pepper and cook for 1 minute more. Serve immediately.

Variations: Add 1 cup halved cherry tomatoes and ½ cup plain bread crumbs with the zucchini.

Broiled Sesame Eggplant

Use small, violet-colored Japanese eggplants for the best flavor. This dish can be served hot or at room temperature.

Preparation time: 15 minutes
Storage: 2 days refrigerated
Serves 2–4

2 slender Japanese eggplants, halved lengthwise

2 tablespoons olive oil

Salt and freshly ground pepper to taste

1 tablespoon Asian sesame oil

4 teaspoons sesame seeds

1 tablespoon tamari

1 garlic clove, minced

1. Preheat the broiler. Line a baking sheet with foil.

2. Brush the cut sides of the eggplants with 1 tablespoon of the olive oil and sprinkle with the salt and pepper. Broil eggplants until they are tender, 3 to 4 minutes per side.

3. Meanwhile, make the dressing: In a small bowl, combine the sesame oil, sesame seeds, tamari, and garlic and salt and pepper to taste. Place the eggplant halves on a serving platter and pour the dressing on top. Serve hot or at room temperature.

Variation: Add a $\frac{1}{4}$-inch slice of ginger, minced or grated, to the dressing.

Eggplant Puree with Basil

Use tender, small eggplants with underdeveloped seeds for this silky puree, which works as well as a dip as it does as a side dish.

Preparation time: 10 minutes
Storage: 2 days refrigerated
Serves 4–6

2 small purple
eggplants, peeled and
cut into ½-inch slices

2 garlic cloves

¼ cup fresh basil leaves

2 tablespoons
extra-virgin olive oil

2 tablespoons olive oil

Salt and freshly ground
pepper to taste

1. Place about 1 inch of water on the bottom of a large pot with a tight-fitting lid. Place the steamer basket in the pot and turn the heat to high. When the water is boiling, add the eggplant slices, cover the pot, and cook until the eggplant is done, 2 to 3 minutes. Remove the steamer basket from the pot.

2. Place the garlic and basil in the bowl of a food processor and process until they are finely chopped. Add the eggplant, olive oil, salt, and pepper and process until the mixture is smooth. Serve hot or at room temperature.

Variations: Add 2 or 3 anchovy fillets and a dash of lemon juice or white wine vinegar to the mixture before pureeing.

Roasted Asparagus

Use coarse sea salt for this extremely simple preparation; it will really enhance the flavor.

Preparation time: 15 minutes
Storage: 2 days refrigerated
Serves 4–6

1 pound thick asparagus, stems snapped

2 tablespoons olive oil

Coarse sea salt to taste

1. Preheat the oven to 450° F.

2. Brush the asparagus with the olive oil and place them in a baking pan. Sprinkle on the salt.

3. Roast the asparagus for 10 to 15 minutes, depending upon how thick the asparagus are. They should be quite soft but not very browned. Serve hot, warm, or at room temperature.

Sautéed Cherry Tomatoes

Use the sweetest, ripest cherry tomatoes you can find.

Preparation time: 10 minutes
Storage: 2 days refrigerated
Serves 4

2 tablespoons extra-virgin olive oil	2 tablespoons chopped fresh basil
1 pint cherry tomatoes, stemmed if necessary	Salt and freshly ground pepper to taste

1. In a large pan over medium-high heat, heat the olive oil until it is hot but not smoking. Add the tomatoes and sauté until they are wilted, about 3 minutes.

2. Stir in the basil, salt, and pepper and serve immediately.

Variations: Add 1 cup of cubed fresh mozzarella or brie cheese to this dish just before serving. The cheese will melt ever so slightly, and the result is really terrific.

Sautéed Radicchio

Preparation time: 10 minutes

Storage: None

Serves 4

2 tablespoons
extra-virgin olive oil

2 heads radicchio,
cored and shredded

Salt and freshly ground
pepper to taste

1. In a large pan heat the olive oil over medium-high heat until it is hot but not smoking. Add the radicchio and sauté until it is wilted, about 3 minutes.

2. Stir in the salt and pepper and serve immediately.

Variations: For Walnut Sautéed Radicchio, replace the olive oil with walnut oil and garnish the dish with ⅓ cup chopped walnuts.

Braised Kale

This fat-free, vitamin-packed dish is now a standard at my Thanksgiving dinner, which marks the true beginning of the kale season. In fact, not only do we consume the frilly green, we also decorate with it. The centerpiece is invariably a tricolored head of kale, brilliant in its cream, green, and purple ruffles.

Preparation time: 10 minutes
Storage: None
Serves 6

½ cup chicken broth	1 pound kale, trimmed and chopped
2 garlic cloves, smashed	Salt and freshly ground pepper to taste

1. In a large pan heat the chicken broth and garlic over medium heat until the broth begins to steam. Add the kale and sauté until it is wilted and tender, 4 to 5 minutes.

2. Stir in the salt and pepper and serve immediately.

Balsamic Pearl Onions and Raisins

This sweet-and-sour dish showcases pearl onions. They look impressive but are easy to prepare thanks to the frozen kind, which eliminate the usual peeling and blanching.

This is another Thanksgiving favorite. Use the leftovers as a relish to put on turkey sandwiches.

Preparation time: 15 minutes
Storage: 5 days refrigerated
Serves 6–8

3 tablespoons butter	2 whole cloves
2 cups frozen pearl onions	2 tablespoons balsamic vinegar
1 cup dark raisins	Salt and freshly ground pepper to taste
2 tablespoons sugar	
1 bay leaf	

1. In a large pan melt the butter over medium-high heat. When the foam subsides, add the onions, raisins, sugar, bay leaf, and cloves. Cook the mixture, stirring, until the onions are lightly caramelized, about 7 minutes.

2. Stir in the balsamic vinegar, salt, and pepper and serve immediately. Or, for added elegance, fish out the bay leaf and cloves before serving.

Sugar Snap Peas with Mint and Cream

Preparation time: 10 minutes

Storage: none

Serves 6

1 pound sugar snap peas, trimmed	¼ cup chopped fresh mint
3 tablespoons heavy cream	Salt and freshly ground pepper to taste
2 tablespoons butter	

1. Bring a large pot of water to a boil. Add the peas and cook until they are done to your taste. (I cook them for about 2 minutes total.) Drain and refresh under cold water.

2. While the peas are cooking, make the sauce: In a small saucepan over high heat, combine the cream and butter. Cook the mixture until it reduces and thickens, about 2 minutes. Stir in the mint, salt, and pepper.

3. Place the peas in a large serving bowl. Pour on the sauce and toss to combine.

Variations: My friend Ana Deboo served me Sugar Snap Peas with Mint and Balsamic Vinegar at a memorable dinner one spring evening. Dinner consisted of a tremendous bowl of peas, a huge green salad, and a rhubarb and strawberry pie made with brown sugar for dessert. We didn't need anything more! To make the peas, omit the butter and cream and toss the peas instead with the mint and 2 tablespoons balsamic vinegar.

Hot Chickpeas Vinaigrette

This makes a fine salad when served on a bed of tender young spinach, which will wilt under the heat of the chickpeas.

Preparation time: 10 minutes
Storage: None
Serves 6

⅓ cup olive oil

2 garlic cloves, minced

3 tablespoons tarragon vinegar or lemon juice

2 cans (16 ounces each) chickpeas, rinsed

2 tablespoons chopped red onion

2 tablespoons chopped fresh Italian parsley

Salt and freshly ground pepper to taste

1. In a small pan over medium-high heat, heat the olive oil until it is hot but not smoking. Add the garlic and turn off the heat.

2. In a large serving bowl, combine the garlic oil, vinegar, chickpeas, onion, parsley, salt, and pepper. Toss to combine and serve immediately.

sorbets and ice creams

Lemon Curd Ice Cream

Lemon curd provides the richness of egg yolks without any effort. It is a superior dessert worthy of your most important guests, as are the variations.

For this recipe, as for all the others that call for lemon curd, use the very best you can find, such as Tiptree or Master Choice (see Sources, page vi).

Preparation time: 5 minutes, plus freezing
Storage: 2 weeks frozen
Makes about 1 pint

1 cup heavy cream	1 jar (about 11 ounces) lemon curd

1. Combine the ingredients in the bowl of an ice cream maker.

2. Freeze according to the manufacturer's instructions.

Variations: For Lemon Clove Ice Cream, simply add $\frac{1}{4}$ teaspoon ground cloves to the mixture before freezing. This is a wonderful pairing. For Lemon Curd–Raspberry Parfait, spoon 1 tablespoon of Luscious Raspberry Sauce (page 229) in the bottom of each parfait glass or wineglass. Add a small scoop of Lemon Curd Ice Cream, then top with another tablespoon of sauce. Add a final scoop of the ice cream and drizzle on 2 tablespoons of the sauce. Serve with or without whipped cream.

Julian Clark's Maple Pecan Ice Cream

This ice cream recipe, developed by my father, makes an excellent dessert, especially when served with a bit of maple syrup drizzled over the top.

Preparation time: 5 minutes, plus freezing
Storage: 2 weeks frozen
Makes about 1 quart

2 cups maple syrup	1 cup plain yogurt
1 cup heavy cream	¾ cup coarsely chopped pecans

1. Combine the ingredients in the bowl of an ice cream maker.

2. Freeze according to the manufacturer's instructions.

Grape Ice Cream

Preparation time: 5 minutes, plus freezing
Storage: 5 days frozen
Makes about 1 pint

1 cup heavy cream

¾ cup grape juice
concentrate

1. Combine the ingredients in the bowl of an ice cream maker.

2. Freeze according to the manufacturer's instructions.

Quick Lime Ice Cream

Preparation time: 10 minutes, plus freezing
Storage: 2 weeks frozen
Makes about 1 pint

Grated zest
of 2 limes

¼ cup superfine sugar

1 cup heavy cream

1 cup frozen
limeade concentrate

1. Combine the ingredients in the bowl of an ice cream maker.

2. Freeze according to the manufacturer's instructions.

Mulled Wine Sorbet

Enjoy this winter favorite as it has been transformed into a sublime frozen form. You may omit the cardamom if you cannot find whole cardamom pods; the ground version is too bitter for this recipe. For a slightly caramelized flavor, use dark brown sugar instead of granulated sugar.

For a memorable dessert (which is, incidentally, fat-free), serve a small scoop of this sorbet with the Roasted Pears with Star Anise (page 221).

Preparation time: 10 minutes, plus cooling and freezing
Storage: 2 weeks frozen
Makes about 1 pint

2 cups red wine

2 whole cloves

½ teaspoon ground cinnamon

½ teaspoon ground ginger

½ teaspoon freshly ground cardamom

2-inch strip of orange zest

½ cup sugar, or to taste

1. Combine all the ingredients in a heavy-bottomed saucepan over medium heat. Stir until the sugar dissolves, about 5 minutes.

2. Refrigerate wine mixture until cool. Then freeze in an ice cream maker according to the manufacturer's instructions.

Ginger-Pineapple Frozen Yogurt

This is about as creamy and delicious as fat-free gets. Serve it with Apricot Lace Cookies (page 225) or Crispy Caramel Palmiers (page 224).

Preparation time: 5 minutes, plus freezing
Storage: 3 weeks, frozen
Makes about 1 quart

1 can (20 ounces)
crushed pineapple
in syrup

1 pint nonfat plain
or vanilla yogurt

¼ cup preserved ginger
or ginger preserves

1 teaspoon
ground ginger

Superfine sugar to
taste (optional)

1. Combine all the ingredients in a large bowl. Mix well to combine. Taste the mixture, and if it seems too tart, add some superfine sugar.

2. Freeze the mixture in an ice cream maker according to the manufacturer's instructions.

Apricot Honey Sorbet

Thanks to the honey, this is a luscious, creamy sorbet. Use a good brand of apricot nectar.

Preparation time: 5 minutes, plus freezing
Storage: 2 weeks frozen
Makes about 1 pint

2 cups apricot nectar	1 teaspoon lemon juice
¼ cup honey	Dash of almond extract

1. Combine all the ingredients in the bowl of an ice cream maker.

2. Freeze according to the manufacturer's instructions.

Peach-Cassis Sorbet

This light, fruity sorbet has a slightly icy texture that you can easily smooth out by adding 1 beaten egg white to the mixture.

As for buying the peach nectar and cassis juice, the former will be easy to find, especially if you live near a Hispanic market that sells Goya products. Looza, available at gourmet-type stores, makes both a peach nectar and a cassis juice, and they are excellent.

Preparation time: 5 minutes
Storage: 2 weeks frozen
Makes about 1 quart

$1\frac{1}{2}$ **cups peach nectar**

2 cups cassis juice

1 tablespoon crème de cassis

1. Combine all the ingredients in the bowl of an ice cream maker.

2. Freeze according to the manufacturer's instructions.

Green Apple Sorbet

This lively sorbet is perfectly complemented by sweetened, cinnamon-flavored whipped cream. As for the frozen Granny Smith apple juice concentrate, Seneca makes it, and it should be available in most supermarkets.

Preparation time: 5 minutes, plus freezing
Storage: 3 weeks frozen
Makes about 1 pint

> 1 package (12 ounces)
> frozen Granny Smith
> apple juice concentrate

> 6 tablespoons
> superfine sugar
>
> ½ cup water

1. Combine all ingredients in a large bowl and stir until the sugar is dissolved.

2. Freeze in an ice cream maker according to the manufacturer's instructions.

Coffee Granita

Although I find granitas more troublesome to make than sorbets (they need attention every thirty minutes or so), they have the distinct advantage of being made without an ice cream maker. Any of these recipes can also be frozen in an ice cream maker to make a sorbet, but they won't have that icy, granular texture that makes granitas so special.

This is a traditional Italian recipe that should replace the coffee break on summery afternoons.

Preparation time: 5 minutes, plus freezing

Storage: 2–3 days frozen

Makes about 1 pint

2 cups hot, strong coffee   **6 tablespoons sugar**

1. In a small bowl, stir together the coffee and the sugar until the sugar dissolves.

2. Pour the mixture into a shallow metal pan (an 8- or 9-inch cake pan is perfect) and freeze the mixture for about 3 hours, stirring every half hour, until it is slushy and frozen.

3. Serve immediately, or freeze for 2 to 3 days and thaw for 15 minutes before serving.

Earl Grey Tea Granita

A wonderfully fragrant granita that is not too sweet.

Preparation time: 5 minutes, plus freezing

Storage: 2–3 days frozen

Makes about 1 pint

2 cups strong,   **3 to 4 tablespoons sugar,**
hot Earl Grey tea   **or to taste**

1. In a small bowl, combine the tea and the sugar, stirring well to dissolve the sugar.

2. Pour the mixture into a shallow metal pan (an 8- or 9-inch cake pan is perfect) and freeze the mixture for about 3 hours, stirring every half hour, until it is slushy and frozen.

3. Serve immediately, or freeze for 2 to 3 days and thaw for 15 minutes before serving.

desserts

Free-Form Plum Almond Tart

A simple, seasonal tart that lends itself well to variation. Try substituting apples or pears for the plums in the fall and winter, and peaches in the early summer. Or use frozen sliced peaches and make this tart anytime.

Make sure to use puff pastry made with butter for this and all other puff pastry recipes. It makes a tremendous difference.

Preparation time: 20 minutes, plus baking
Storage: Serve on day baked
Serves 6–8

8 ounces frozen puff pastry, thawed for 20 minutes	⅓ cup sliced, blanched almonds
2 cups pitted and sliced fresh plums	¼ teaspoon almond extract
1 large egg	2 tablespoons milk, for brushing crust
⅓ cup sugar	

1. Preheat the oven to 375° F.

2. Open the sheet of puff pastry and flatten out the seams with your palms. The puff pastry should be square or rectangular in shape. Place the puff pastry on a baking

sheet. You could trim the corners of the puff pastry, if desired, or leave them and fold them over the fruit once the tart is filled. Refrigerate puff pastry until needed.

3. In a bowl, mix the plums, egg, sugar, almonds, and almond extract until well combined. Spoon this mixture onto the puff pastry, leaving a 1-inch border around the sides.

4. Fold the sides of the puff pastry over the filling to partially enclose it. Do not worry if it looks lumpy or messy; the aim is simply to keep the filling from running off the pastry. Puff pastry is extremely forgiving, and while it bakes, the crust will metamorphose into something golden brown and rustically beautiful.

5. Using either a pastry brush or your fingers, dab the crust with milk. Place the tart in the oven and bake until the crust is golden brown and the filling bubbly and fragrant, 30 to 40 minutes. Serve warm or at room temperature.

Variations: Substitute chopped hazelnuts or walnuts for the almonds. Replace the granulated sugar with brown sugar and add a few dashes of cinnamon. Substitute sliced apples, pears, apricots, or peaches for the plums.

Caramelized Pineapple Tart

Make sure to use all-butter puff pastry for this delectable tart, which is well enhanced with a dab of Rum Cream (page 231) served alongside.

If you can find ripe, fresh sliced pineapple (or slice it yourself), do use it; the tart will be all the tastier!

Preparation time: 20 minutes, plus baking

Storage: Pineapple keeps 3 days refrigerated

Serves 6

8 ounces frozen puff pastry, thawed for 20 minutes	**6 slices canned pineapple (no sugar added)**
¼ cup caramel sauce, prepared or homemade (page 227)	**1 tablespoon Cognac (optional)**

1. Lay the puff pastry out on a baking sheet, smoothing away any creases in the dough. If you are not yet ready to bake, lay a piece of plastic wrap over the dough and refrigerate for up to 3 hours.

2. When you are ready to bake, preheat the oven to 400° F.

3. In a large skillet over medium heat, melt the caramel sauce. Add the pineapple slices and cook them for about 3 minutes, just long enough for them to absorb the sauce. Stir in the Cognac, if desired, and remove the pan from the heat.

4. Place the pineapple slices in caramel sauce, overlapping, on top of the tart shell. Make sure to leave a 1-inch border. Fold the pastry over the pineapple to enclose it. Don't worry about how the tart looks; it will be gorgeous once baked. If you wish, you can trim the corners of the pastry or you can just fold them over.

5. Bake the tart until the crust is golden, 30 to 35 minutes. Serve immediately.

Variations: Sprinkle on a dash or two of ground cinnamon or nutmeg, or chop 1 to 2 tablespoons of candied ginger and add that to the pineapple.

Pumpkin Butter Tart with Pecans and Raisins

Serve this autumnal tart with large dollops of Bourbon Cream (page 229). It makes a perfect Thanksgiving dessert.

Preparation time: 10 minutes, plus baking
Storage: None
Serves: 6–8

8 ounces frozen puff pastry, thawed for 20 minutes

1 cup pumpkin butter

¼ cup golden raisins

¼ cup pecans

1. Preheat the oven to 375° F.

2. Open the sheet of puff pastry and flatten out the seams with your palms. The puff pastry should be square or rectangular in shape. Place the puff pastry on the greased baking sheet. You could trim the corners of the puff pastry, if desired, or leave them and fold them over once the tart is filled.

3. Spread the pumpkin butter over the puff pastry, leaving a 1-inch border. Sprinkle the raisins and pecans over the pumpkin butter.

4. Fold the sides of the puff pastry over the filling to partially enclose it. Do not worry if it looks lumpy or messy; the aim is simply to keep the filling from running off the pastry. Puff pastry is extremely forgiving, and while it bakes, the crust will metamorphose into something golden brown and rustically beautiful.

5. Place the tart in the oven and bake until the crust is golden brown, 30 to 35 minutes. Serve while still warm.

Free-Form Raspberry and Fresh Fig Tart

Wait for autumn to supply a windfall of fresh figs before making this tart. It is well worth the wait.

Preparation time: 15 minutes, plus baking
Storage: Serve on day baked, preferably warm from oven
Serves 6

9-inch sheet
ready-made pie dough

1 cup fresh raspberries

6 fresh figs,
in ¼-inch slices

3 tablespoons sugar

1 tablespoon
melted butter

1. Preheat the oven to 400° F.

2. Lay the pie dough out on a baking sheet, smoothing away any creases with your hands.

3. In a medium bowl, place the raspberries, figs, sugar, and melted butter, tossing to combine.

4. Place the fruit filling on top of the pie dough, leaving a 1½-inch border. Fold up the border over the fruit. Don't worry about it being neat; the purpose here is to keep the filling from running all over the pan.

5. Bake the tart until the crust is golden brown and the filling bubbling, about 30 minutes. Serve warm.

Variations: For a Blueberry Fig Tart, substitute blueberries for the raspberries, or use all raspberries or all figs.

Ricotta Tart with Marsala

If you are really pressed for time and want to skip prebaking the crust, you could bake this as a cheesecake in a nine-inch springform pan without a pastry.

Preparation time: 15 minutes, plus baking
Storage: Serve on day baked
Serves 8–10

9-inch sheet ready-made pie dough	1¼ cups ricotta cheese
1½ cups sugar	4 large eggs, lightly beaten
4 ounces cream cheese, softened	½ cup Marsala or sherry

1. Preheat oven to 375° F. Fit the pie dough into a 9-inch tart pan with a removable bottom, folding any overhanging dough back into the pan to build up the sides of the tart. Prick the bottom of the tart shell with a fork, then line it with aluminum foil. Fill foil with pie weights, dried beans, rice, or pennies. Bake the tart shell for 10 minutes. Remove foil and weights, then bake for 5 minutes more.

2. In a food processor fitted with a steel blade, process the sugar for 30 seconds. Add the other ingredients and process until smooth and creamy, 20 seconds more.

3. Pour the filling into the pie shell. Lower the oven temperature to 350° F. Bake the tart until the edges are set but the center is still slightly wobbly, 35 to 40 minutes. Cool completely before serving.

Variations: For a Raisin Ricotta Tart, marinate ⅓ cup raisins in the Marsala for 1 hour. Quickly process the mixture into the filling.

Orange Zest Truffle Tart

This dense pie is like eating chocolate truffles in a crust, only a bit lighter. For a pure chocolate experience, omit the orange zest and Grand Marnier.

Preparation time: 15 minutes, plus baking
Storage: Serve on day baked; keeps overnight at room temperature
Serves 8–10

9-inch sheet ready-made
pie dough

1 cup half-and-half

6 ounces bittersweet
chocolate,
finely chopped

1 teaspoon grated orange zest

1 large egg, lightly beaten

2 tablespoons
Grand Marnier (optional)

1. Preheat the oven to 350° F. Fit the pie dough into a 9-inch tart pan with a removable bottom, folding any overhanging dough back into the pan to build up the sides of the tart. Prick the bottom of the tart shell with a fork, then line it with aluminum foil. Fill foil with pie weights, dried beans, rice, or pennies. Bake tart shell for 10 minutes. Remove foil and weights. Bake for 5 minutes more.

2. Meanwhile, scald (heat to just below the boiling point) the half-and-half. Remove pan from heat. Stir in the chocolate and orange zest and continue stirring until the mixture is very smooth and the chocolate melted. When the mixture has cooled somewhat, stir in the egg and Grand Marnier, if using.

3. Pour the filling into the tart shell and return to the oven. Bake until the filling is just set, about 15 minutes. Do not overcook. Remove the tart to a wire rack and let cool. Serve warm or at room temperature.

Peach Tarte Tatin

Understanding how to make a proper tarte tatin is the key to pastry freedom. It's so easy, and takes so well to variations, that once you know the technique of caramelizing the sugar and inverting the tart, you can improvise as far as your imagination takes you. Serve this with whipped cream or vanilla ice cream.

Preparation time: 15 minutes, plus baking
Storage: None
Serves 6–8

¾ cup sugar

½ cup butter, cut into small pieces

3 cups sliced frozen peaches

9-inch sheet ready-made pie dough

1. Preheat the oven to 350° F.

2. In a 10-inch ovenproof skillet, heat the sugar over low heat until it begins to melt. Cook the sugar, stirring up any lumps, until it turns golden brown. Remove pan from heat.

3. Scatter the butter pieces over the sugar. Place the peach slices decoratively on top of the butter. Cover the peaches with the pie dough, tucking the edges around the fruit.

4. Bake the tart until the pastry is golden brown and the peaches are cooked, 30 to 35 minutes. Remove the tart from the oven and let cool slightly. Using a small, sharp knife, loosen the pastry from the skillet. Invert the tart onto a serving platter and serve immediately.

Variations: For a Classic Tarte Tatin, substitute sliced, peeled apples for the peaches. For a Pear Tarte Tatin, use sliced, peeled pears. For a Banana Tarte Tatin, use 7 large bananas, sliced into rounds.

Chocolate Fudge Pie

This incredibly dense, rich, moist pie is God's gift to the sweet-toothed. Serve it with whipped cream.

Preparation time: 15 minutes, plus baking
Storage: Serve on day baked
Serves 8–10

1 ready-made 9-inch pie shell

½ cup (1 stick) butter

1½ cups sugar

2 ounces bittersweet
chocolate,
finely chopped

1 tablespoon vinegar
or lemon juice

3 large eggs, lightly beaten

1 teaspoon vanilla extract

Pinch of salt

1. Preheat the oven to 375° F. Prick pie shell with a fork, then line dough with foil. Fill with pie weights or dried beans and bake for 15 minutes. Remove the foil and the weights. Bake for another 10 minutes. Remove crust to a wire rack to cool slightly.

2. Meanwhile, prepare the filling. In a medium saucepan, melt the butter with the sugar, stirring until the sugar is dissolved. Remove the pan from the heat; add the chocolate and stir until it is completely melted. Stir in the vinegar, eggs, vanilla, and salt.

3. Lower the oven temperature to 325°. Pour the filling into the pie crust. Bake the pie until the filling is just set and the crust golden, about 40 minutes.

Variations: For a Toasted Almond Fudge Pie, add ¼ teaspoon almond extract and ¾ cup chopped toasted almonds to the filling. For a Chocolate-Mint Fudge Pie, add ¼ teaspoon mint extract. For a Mocha Fudge Pie, add 1 teaspoon espresso powder dissolved in 1 tablespoon hot water.

Chestnut Rum Mousse

A simple, luscious dessert. Serve this with chocolate truffle squares for a memorable finale.

Crème de marron is a sweetened chestnut puree available in most large supermarkets and specialty shops.

Preparation time: 10 minutes
Storage: 3 days refrigerated, but best within 4 hours
Serves 6–8

1 cup heavy cream

1 cup crème de marron

2 tablespoons rum
or 1 teaspoon vanilla extract

1. In a large bowl, beat the heavy cream until it is thick and fluffy.

2. Carefully fold in the crème de marron, taking care not to deflate the cream.

3. Add the rum or vanilla extract.

4. Chill the mousse for at least 30 minutes and up to 4 hours before serving.

Variation: To make Chocolate Chestnut Mousse, simply fold in $\frac{1}{2}$ cup chopped bittersweet chocolate.

English Cream

Although in our immediate family we call this luscious dessert English Cream, the designation of my mother's recipe is quite complicated. At a French gourmet dinner, the pale quivering mold became crème à la Française. At an anniversary party I catered, where the hostess had requested a mousse, it became cream mousse. The recipe really seems to me to be an easy variation on Bavarian cream, so sometimes I call it that. But the best name of all was invented for my friend Elena Stanger's bat mitzvah. My mother called it Jewish cream.

Also, if you chill the mixture in a pretty bowl, don't bother unmolding it, which I do only for special occasions.

Preparation time: 10 minutes, plus 3 hours chilling
Storage: 24 hours refrigerated, but unmolded at serving time
Serves 10–12

2 cups heavy cream	2 tablespoons rum, Cognac, orange juice, or water
1 cup sugar	
1 envelope unflavored gelatin	2 cups sour cream

1. In a heavy, medium saucepan over low heat, combine the cream and sugar. Stir the mixture until the sugar dissolves and the cream is warm. (If the cream gets hot, let it cool until it is warm.)

2. In a small bowl, dissolve the gelatin in the rum. Pour the gelatin mixture into the warm cream and stir to fully dissolve the gelatin. Stir in the sour cream, using a wire whisk or a fork, until the mixture is perfectly smooth.

3. Pour the mixture into an oiled 6-cup mold or a large, pretty bowl. Chill until firm, about 4 hours.

Variation: To make Rose Cream, use rose water instead of the rum and garnish the cream with chopped, candied rose petals (which are available at specialty shops).

Raspberry Honey Ricotta Cream

This lovely cream has the texture of a rich, dense mousse but the fresh flavor of berries. It can be served on its own in small portions, but it is best served with a topping of fresh berries or other fresh fruit. Or make it into a parfait with crumbled shortbread cookies, fresh berries, and luscious Raspberry Sauce (page 229) or Chocolate Sauce (page 230).

Raspberry creamed honey is simply creamed honey mixed with raspberries. It is available in most supermarkets, or by mail order from Dean & DeLuca (see Sources, page vi).

Preparation time: 5 minutes
Storage: 4 days refrigerated
Serves 6

| 1 container (15 ounces) | ¼ cup raspberry |
| ricotta cheese | creamed honey |

1. In a food processor fitted with a steel blade, process the ricotta and honey until the mixture is perfectly smooth, 1 to 2 minutes.

2. Serve immediately, or chill until serving time.

Variations: For a spicy version, add a dash of nutmeg, cinnamon, clove, or ginger to the ricotta mixture.

To make Ginger Orange Ricotta Cream, substitute 1 tablespoon ginger marmalade for 1 tablespoon of the honey, and substitute orange creamed honey for the raspberry. Add 1 to 2 teaspoons Grand Marnier and/or grated orange zest.

Sour Cherry Fool

If you can find it, use American Spoon Foods' wonderful sour cherry spoon fruit for the best results. Serve this on its own or layered in a parfait with Avocado Mousse (page 217). It's a terrific flavor combination, and the colors—pale pink and green—are almost unreal.

Preparation time: 5 minutes, plus chilling
Storage: 3 days refrigerated
Serves 4–6

| ¾ cup heavy cream | 1 cup sour cherry spoon |
| | fruit or preserves |

1. Place the cream in a food processor fitted with a steel blade. Process until it begins to thicken, 20 to 30 seconds; be careful not to overprocess or it will turn to butter.

2. Add the preserves and process until the mixture is thick and creamy and the cherries are chopped, 10 to 20 seconds. Chill the mixture for at least 30 minutes before serving.

Variation: For Chocolate Cherry Fool, add 2 ounces finely chopped bittersweet chocolate.

Avocado Mousse

I first learned that avocados taste wonderful when sweetened and flavored with kirsch after reading an M.F.K. Fisher story in which a man at a fancy California restaurant orders half an avocado for dessert. The waiter serves it with confectioners' sugar and kirsch. I simply made this idea into a creamy mousse, which tastes rich and good on its own but also makes an unusual and delightful filling for a simple butter layer cake or sponge cake.

Preparation time: 5 minutes
Storage: 3 days refrigerated
Serves 4

2 ripe avocados, peeled and pitted	10 tablespoons confectioners' sugar
$\frac{2}{3}$ cup heavy cream	2 tablespoons kirsch

1. Drop the avocados into the bowl of a food processor and process until smooth.

2. Add the remaining ingredients and process until thick and creamy, about 1 minute. Serve immediately or store airtight in the refrigerator.

Variation: For Avocado-Lime Mousse, substitute a combination of fresh lime juice and triple sec or Grand Marnier for the kirsch.

Chocolate-Hazelnut Mousse

When I was a child, my favorite snack was Nutella, a chocolate hazelnut spread. This easy mousse uses my childhood favorite in a very sophisticated manner.

Preparation time: 5 minutes
Storage: 3 days refrigerated
Serves 6–8

2 cups heavy cream

¾ cup chocolate
hazelnut spread

2 teaspoons Cognac
or rum (optional)

1. Whip the cream using an electric mixer or a food processor until it is thick.

2. Fold in the chocolate spread and the Cognac, if desired.

Variations: To add a bittersweet note to this mousse, fold in 2 ounces finely chopped bittersweet chocolate. If you happen to have some Frangelico (a hazelnut liqueur), use it in place of the Cognac.

Roasted Orange Strawberries

Roasting fruit condenses its sweetness and intensifies its natural flavor. I recommend this treatment especially for strawberries out of season, although it makes ripe strawberries taste even richer.

Serve these strawberries at room temperature over ice cream or yogurt or by themselves.

Preparation time: 10 minutes
Storage: 2 days refrigerated
Serves 4

1 pint large, ripe strawberries, hulled

1 tablespoon orange juice

1 tablespoon Grand Marnier

2 tablespoons sugar

1 tablespoon butter, cut into small pieces

1. Preheat the oven to 400° F. Arrange the strawberries in a baking dish large enough to hold them in 1 layer.

2. Drizzle the orange juice and Grand Marnier over the strawberries, then sprinkle on the sugar. Dot with the butter.

3. Roast the strawberries until they are soft and fragrant, about 7 minutes.

Spiced-Wine Poached Grapes

This sublime mixture is really worth buying all the ingredients, should you not have a vanilla bean and star anise in the cupboard. It is absolutely wonderful when served with the English Cream (page 214). But I like it best by itself, with a crisp cookie on the side.

Preparation time: 20 minutes, plus chilling
Storage: 5 days refrigerated
Serves 10

1 bottle white wine	1 bay leaf
1 cup sugar	Pinch of salt
1 vanilla bean, sliced lengthwise	5 peppercorns
4 star anise pods	2½ pounds seedless red grapes, stemmed

1. In a large saucepan over high heat, combine all the ingredients except the grapes. Bring the liquid to a simmer and cook, stirring occasionally, until the sugar dissolves and the liquid thickens slightly, 5 to 6 minutes.

2. Reduce the heat to medium and add the grapes. Cook the mixture until the grapes are soft and withered and the liquid is reduced to a syrup, about 10 minutes.

3. Chill the grapes in the refrigerator until serving time.

Roasted Pears with Star Anise

Star anise is available by mail order from Dean & DeLuca and can also be found in large supermarkets and gourmet stores. It really adds a surprising licorice flavor to these sweet pears.

Preparation time: 15 minutes, plus baking
Storage: Best served while still warm; will keep 3 days, refrigerated
Serves 4

4 ripe Bosc pears	6 star anise
4 teaspoons sugar	1 vanilla bean, split lengthwise

1. Preheat the oven to 350° F. Peel the pears and, using a small, sharp knife, cut a small slice off the bottom of each so that the pears can stand upright.

2. Place the pears on a large piece of aluminum foil and sprinkle each pear with 1 teaspoon of the sugar. Sprinkle the star anise over the pears.

3. Using the tip of a small, sharp knife, scrape the vanilla bean seeds out of the pod over the pears. Place the pod around the pears and draw up the foil to completely enclose the fruit. If your piece of foil is not large enough, cover the pears with another piece of foil and twist up the ends to make a large foil envelope.

4. Bake the pears until they are easily pierced with a fork, about 1 hour. Serve warm or at room temperature.

Moroccan Oranges

This is one of the most refreshing winter desserts I know. Serve it after a large, heavy meal and it will revive you and your guests.

Preparation time: 10 minutes, plus chilling
Storage: 2 days refrigerated
Serves 6

6 navel oranges

¼ cup finely chopped toasted pistachio nuts

¼ cup finely chopped dates (optional)

1 tablespoon confectioners' sugar

2 tablespoons orange-flower water, Cognac, or orange juice

1. Using a small, sharp knife, cut off all the skin, including the bitter white pith. Slice the oranges crosswise into thin slices. Place them on a serving platter.

2. Sprinkle the pistachio nuts and dates over the oranges. Sprinkle on the confectioners' sugar and the orange-flower water. Chill the oranges until ready to serve, at least 30 minutes.

Fresh Berries in Peppered Balsamic Vinegar

Use superfine sugar for this dessert; it melts instantly into the berries.

Preparation time: 5 minutes, plus steeping
Storage: 1 day at room temperature
Serves 4

**2 cups fresh berries
(raspberries, strawberries,
blueberries, or a combination)**

2 teaspoons balsamic vinegar

**Freshly ground
pepper to taste**

Superfine sugar to taste

1. Combine all the ingredients in a small bowl.

2. Let sit for at least 10 minutes before serving. Serve in pretty glasses.

Chocolate-Cognac Truffle Squares

These rich, creamy squares are an ideal dessert for chocolate lovers. Just make sure to make them several hours (or a few days) in advance, so they have time to set.

Preparation time: 10 minutes, plus chilling
Storage: 7 days refrigerated
Makes 36 squares

**12 ounces bittersweet
chocolate, chopped, or
chocolate chips**

1½ cups heavy cream

**2 teaspoons Cognac
(optional)**

1. Place the chocolate in a medium bowl and set aside.

2. In a small saucepan or in the microwave, scald the cream (heat until small bubbles appear around the edges). Immediately pour the hot cream over the chocolate bits and stir until the chocolate has melted and the mixture is smooth.

3. Stir in the Cognac if using.

4. Pour the truffle mixture into a shallow dish and refrigerate until set. This will take several hours.

5. When the mixture is set, cut the truffles into small squares and remove from the pan. Either serve immediately or store in the refrigerator for up to 1 week, tightly wrapped.

Variations: Add $\frac{1}{2}$ cup chopped pecans, walnuts, or hazelnuts to the mixture. Or add dried fruit such as chopped apricots, raisins, chopped prunes, or sour cherries.

Crispy Caramel Palmiers

Packaged puff pastry has to be one of the biggest boons for the hurried baker. Use the all-butter kind for the best flavor and highest rise.

Preparation time: 15 minutes, plus chilling and baking
Storage: 3 days airtight
Makes about 3 dozen

$\frac{1}{2}$ **pound puff pastry,** **thawed for 20 minutes**	**1 cup sugar**

1. Line 2 baking sheets with waxed paper.

2. On a lightly floured surface, roll the puff pastry into an 18 x 11-inch rectangle, about $\frac{1}{8}$ inch thick. Sprinkle the surface with the sugar. Starting with a long end, roll up the dough, jelly-roll style, to the middle of the pastry. Then roll up the other side so they meet in the middle. Cut $\frac{1}{2}$-inch slices and place them on the prepared baking sheets. Flatten each palmier slightly with your hand, then refrigerate for 20 minutes.

3. Preheat the oven to 400° F. Bake the palmiers until golden brown, about 12 minutes.

Variations: To make cinnamon palmiers, sprinkle the puff pastry with cinnamon sugar made from 1 cup sugar mixed with 1 teaspoon ground cinnamon.

Apricot Lace Cookies

Preparation Time: 5 minutes plus baking
Storage: 3 days airtight; waxed paper between layers
Makes 1½ dozen cookies

¼ **cup rolled oats**

2 tablespoons apricot jam

2 tablespoons brown sugar

3 tablespoons butter or margarine

2 tablespoons flour

Dash of salt

1. Preheat the oven to 350° F. Grease 2 or 3 baking sheets.

2. In a small saucepan, combine the oats, jam, brown sugar, and butter. Heat the mixture over medium heat, stirring constantly, until it comes to a boil. Remove from the heat.

3. Stir in the flour and salt until well combined.

4. Spoon ½ teaspoons of the batter onto the prepared baking sheets, leaving at least 2 inches between cookies. Bake the cookies for 8 minutes, or until the edges are lightly browned. Let cookies cool on the baking sheets for a few minutes before removing to a rack to finish cooling.

Variations: For Raspberry Nut Lace Cookies, substitute raspberry jam for the apricot, and chopped nuts for the oats.

Caramelized Bananas

These bananas are terrifically easy and very tasty. Serve them with Luscious Raspberry Sauce (page 229), Chocolate Sauce (page 230), or Rum Cream (page 231).

Preparation time: 10 minutes
Storage: None
Serves 2

2 tablespoons butter

2 ripe bananas, peeled
and sliced lengthwise

2 tablespoons brown sugar

1 cup white wine, or
a combination
of ¾ cup water or
orange juice
and ¼ cup rum

1. In a large, preferably nonstick skillet over medium heat, melt the butter.

2. Add the bananas in 1 layer, sprinkle on the sugar, and pour the wine over them. Let the bananas cook until they are soft and caramelized, about 4 minutes, turning them once. Serve immediately.

Caramel Sauce

A rich, easy sauce that will impress your guests even if you are serving just store-bought ice cream.

Preparation time: 15 minutes
Storage: 1 week refrigerated
Makes 1½ cups

½ cup sugar

3 tablespoons water

¾ cup heavy cream

1 tablespoon fresh lemon juice

2 tablespoons butter

1. In a small, heavy saucepan, heat the sugar and water over high heat, stirring, until the sugar melts and turns a rich golden brown, 2 to 3 minutes. Immediately remove the pan from the heat and pour in the cream. The mixture may splatter, but that's okay; just make sure to hold the pan away from you (or place it in a deep kitchen sink) while you pour in the cream.

2. Return the sauce to the stove, and over low heat, stir until the caramel melts and becomes smooth, about 3 minutes.

3. Add the lemon juice and butter and stir until they are absorbed. Serve immediately or store. Reheat in the microwave or over low heat.

Easy Microwave Butterscotch Sauce

The microwave works wonders when cooking sugar. This sticky sauce, perfect for gilding ice cream and fresh peaches, is ready in five minutes and requires absolutely no attention.

Preparation time: 5 minutes
Storage: 1 month refrigerated
Makes 1 cup

1 cup packed light brown sugar	**2 tablespoons butter**
⅓ cup heavy cream	**2 tablespoons light corn syrup**

1. Combine all the ingredients in a 4-cup glass measuring cup and mix well.

2. Cook on high power for 2 minutes. Remove from the microwave and stir well. Serve immediately or store.

Luscious Raspberry Sauce

Preparation time: 15 minutes
Storage: 1 week refrigerated, 6 months frozen
Makes 2½ cups

2 cups frozen raspberries

6 tablespoons sugar

⅓ cup white wine,
orange juice, or water

3 tablespoons
raspberry preserves

1. In a medium saucepan over medium-high heat, combine the raspberries, sugar, wine, and preserves. Cook the mixture, stirring, until it is slightly thickened, 5 to 6 minutes.

2. Remove pan from heat and let the raspberries cool slightly. Puree the sauce in a food processor or blender. Strain the sauce if desired.

Bourbon Cream

Preparation time: 5 minutes
Storage: 2 hours refrigerated
Makes 2 cups

1 cup heavy cream

2 tablespoons bourbon

2 tablespoons sugar

1. Using an electric mixer or by hand, whip the cream until it just begins to thicken.

2. Add the bourbon and the sugar and continue whipping until thick and fluffy. Serve immediately or chill.

Variations: For Rum Cream, substitute rum for the bourbon; for Brandy Cream, substitute brandy.

Chocolate Sauce

If you don't have the inclination to chop up a bar of bittersweet chocolate, use semi-sweet chocolate chips for this rich brown sauce; 3 ounces of chocolate chips is half of a six-ounce bag.

Preparation time: 5 minutes
Storage: Several weeks refrigerated
Makes 1½ cups

½ cup heavy cream

3 ounces bittersweet
chocolate, chopped

1. In a small saucepan scald the cream over medium heat (heat until tiny bubbles appear in the cream around the edges of the saucepan).

2. Remove pan from heat and add the chocolate, stirring until smooth.

3. When ready to use, simply reheat in the microwave or over low heat until melted again.

Variations: This sauce can be flavored with up to 1 tablespoon of Cognac, rum, Grand Marnier, espresso, or Kahlúa. A pinch of ground cinnamon is also a nice addition.

basics

Roasted Garlic

This simple preparation is based on one I found in Barbara Kafka's *Microwave Gourmet*. I usually make this dish using a few teaspoons of *glace de viande*, available frozen, mixed with water, to make the stock, although canned broth is good.

Preparation time: 10 minutes, plus cooling
Storage: 1 week refrigerated
Makes 2 heads

2 heads garlic,
tops sliced off so most
of the cloves are exposed

3 tablespoons chicken
or meat broth

2 tablespoons
olive oil

1 teaspoon

1. Place the garlic in a 6-cup glass measuring cup. Add the chicken broth, olive oil, and vinegar and cover the top with microwavable plastic wrap.

2. Microwave the garlic on high power for 5 minutes.

3. Remove the measuring cup from the microwave and let sit 5 to 7 minutes before uncovering.

Peanut Sauce

This slightly sweet, nutty sauce can be made as hot as you want it by adjusting the amount of hot red pepper flakes. It makes a terrific dip all by itself, and can be incorporated into recipes in this book that call for it.

If you buy canned unsweetened coconut milk at an Asian or Indian market, you will find that the cream will rise to the top (as expected) while the milk rests on the bottom. Drain off this thin, clear milk and use it in the recipe. Of course, water is perfectly fine, and is what I usually use.

Preparation time: 5 minutes
Storage: 1 week refrigerated, 1 month frozen
Makes 2 cups

1⅓ cups unsalted roasted peanuts

1 garlic clove

¼-inch slice of fresh ginger

2 tablespoons tamari

6 fresh basil leaves

Pinch of hot red pepper flakes

Juice of ½ lime

½ cup thin coconut milk (not cream) or warm water

3 tablespoons honey

1. In a food processor fitted with a steel blade, combine the peanuts, garlic, ginger, and basil. Process until everything is finely chopped. Add the remaining ingredients and process until the mixture is fairly, but not completely, smooth. Some small chunks are desirable.

Olivada

The most time-consuming thing about this recipe is pitting the olives. I find that using my fingers is a lot quicker than using an olive pitter. Also, I always use the crinkly black Moroccan olives, since they have the softest flesh and are the easiest to pit. Barbara Kafka has a good olive-pitting trick, which I discuss on page 5.

Don't even think of using the canned pitted black olives from California. The flavor is just not right.

For green olivada, use any type of green olive that you like. I like picholines, but then I usually use the pitted Spanish olives available in bottles. Just don't use the pimento-stuffed kind unless you don't mind a funny brown color in the resulting spread. The flavor is quite nice, though. Also, the almond-stuffed green olives make a wonderful, if nontraditional, spread.

Preparation time: 15 minutes
Storage: 2 weeks or longer refrigerated, 6 months frozen
Makes 1 cup

¾ cup pitted black or green olives

¼ cup extra-virgin olive oil

1 teaspoon lemon juice

1. Process all the ingredients in a food processor fitted with a steel blade. When smooth, place in a jar with a tight-fitting lid and store in the refrigerator.

2. If you are planning to store the olivada for a long period of time, cover the top with a thin layer of olive oil. Every time you use some, replace the olive-oil seal.

Pesto

Here is my basic recipe for pesto, but feel free to alter it to suit your tastes.

Preparation time: 5 minutes
Storage: 6 months frozen
Makes 2 cups

4 garlic cloves

2 cups fresh basil leaves

$\frac{2}{3}$ cup extra-virgin olive oil

3 tablespoons pine nuts or almonds

$\frac{1}{3}$ cup freshly grated parmesan cheese

Salt and freshly ground pepper to taste

Process all the ingredients in a food processor fitted with a steel blade until smooth.

Walnut Pesto

You can make this pesto variation with any herb or combination of herbs you desire. Basil is a good standby, but cilantro, mint, parsley, and watercress are all good substitutes.

Preparation time: 5 minutes
Storage: 6 months frozen
Makes 1 cup

1 cup toasted walnuts	½ cup walnut oil
2 cups fresh herbs	Salt and freshly ground pepper to taste
3 garlic cloves	

Process all the ingredients in a food processor fitted with a steel blade until smooth.

Basic Vinaigrette

Always use the finest extra-virgin olive oil you can afford. It will really set your dressing apart.

Preparation time: 5 minutes
Storage: 1 week refrigerated
Makes scant ⅔ cup

| ½ cup extra-virgin olive oil | 1 tablespoon fresh lemon juice |
| 2 tablespoons red or white wine vinegar or other vinegar | Salt and freshly ground pepper to taste |

1. Mix all the ingredients in a bowl or a jar with a tight-fitting lid.

2. Whisk or shake the vinaigrette until everything is well combined.

Variations: For a Balsamic Vinaigrette, substitute 1 tablespoon balsamic vinegar for the lemon juice. For a Mustard Vinaigrette, substitute 1 teaspoon prepared mustard for the lemon juice. For an Herbed Vinaigrette, add 2 tablespoons of your favorite chopped fresh herbs.

Lemon Vinaigrette

Preparation time: 5 minutes
Storage: 1 week refrigerated
Makes scant ²/₃ cup

½ cup extra-virgin
olive oil

Juice of ½ lemon

Salt and freshly ground
pepper to taste

1. Mix all the ingredients in a bowl or a jar with a tight-fitting lid.

2. Whisk or shake the vinaigrette until everything is well combined.

Soy Sauce Vinaigrette

This is based on a vinaigrette that my associate Bernard Ohlstein used to make. It is simple and wonderful.

Preparation time: 5 minutes
Storage: 1 week refrigerated
Makes scant ²/₃ cup

¹/₂ cup extra-virgin
olive oil

3 tablespoons fresh lemon juice

1 tablespoon soy sauce

1. Mix all the ingredients in a bowl or a jar with a tight-fitting lid.

2. Whisk or shake the vinaigrette until everything is well combined.

Variations: For Sesame-Soy Vinaigrette, substitute 2 tablespoons Asian sesame oil for the olive oil.

Citrus Vinaigrette with Basil

I like to use this slightly sweet vinaigrette on bitter greens, such as arugula, frisée, and watercress.

Preparation time: 5 minutes
Storage: 1 week refrigerated
Makes 1 scant cup

3 tablespoons fresh orange juice

3 tablespoons fresh lemon juice

½ cup olive oil

1 tablespoon minced fresh basil

Salt and freshly ground pepper to taste

1. Mix all the ingredients in a bowl or a jar with a tight-fitting lid.

2. Whisk or shake the vinaigrette until everything is well combined.

Walnut or Hazelnut Vinaigrette

This is probably my favorite of all the vinaigrette variants.

Preparation time: 5 minutes
Storage: 1 week refrigerated
Makes scant ⅔ cup

½ cup walnut or hazelnut oil	2 teaspoons tarragon or white wine vinegar
2 tablespoons lemon juice	Salt and freshly ground pepper to taste

1. Mix all the ingredients in a bowl or a jar with a tight-fitting lid.

2. Whisk or shake the vinaigrette until everything is well combined.

Garlic Vinaigrette

There are many people who do not like garlic in their vinaigrette. Queen Victoria was one, and so her chef, who couldn't resist garlic himself, would pop a whole clove into his mouth, chew, and then exhale over her salad. If you have a wooden salad bowl that hasn't been finished with shellac, you could rub a halved garlic clove on the inside to impart a subtle flavor.

Preparation time: 5 minutes

Storage: None

Makes scant ⅔ cup

½ cup extra-virgin olive oil	**1 garlic clove, finely minced**
2 tablespoons red wine vinegar	**Salt and freshly ground pepper to taste**

1. Mix all the ingredients in a bowl or a jar with a tight-fitting lid.

2. Whisk or shake the vinaigrette until everything is well combined.

Roasted Garlic Vinaigrette

Here is a more refined but no less aromatic version of a garlicky vinaigrette.

Preparation time: 5 minutes

Storage: None

Makes scant ⅔ cup

½ cup extra-virgin olive oil	**4 to 6 roasted garlic cloves, peeled**
2 tablespoons tarragon or white wine vinegar	**Salt and freshly ground pepper to taste**

1. In a food processor or blender, combine all the ingredients.

2. Process until the mixture is smooth.

Caesar Salad Dressing

This is a nontraditional Caesar dressing in that I use the whole egg, lightly cooked, not just the yolk.

Preparation time: 5 minutes
Storage: None
Makes scant ⅔ cup

1 egg

1 large, fat garlic clove

2 tablespoons freshly
grated Parmesan cheese

2 anchovy fillets

1 teaspoon drained capers

¼ cup extra-virgin
olive oil

Juice of ½ lemon

Dash of Worcestershire sauce

Dash of Tabasco

Salt and freshly
ground pepper to taste

1. Bring a small saucepan of water to a boil and cook the egg, in its shell, for 1 to 1½ minutes.

2. Scoop the egg out of the shell and into the bowl of a food processor or blender, add the remaining ingredients, and pulse to combine.

3. Process until the mixture is smooth.

Fresh and Chunky Salsa

You can make this salsa as hot or mild as you wish by adjusting the amount of jalapeño. The fire of any chile is contained in the inner veins, which hold its seeds.

Therefore, either leave the veins in or scrape them away, depending on your taste. No matter what, always wear rubber gloves on your hands when handling chiles.

Preparation time: 10 minutes
Storage: 3 days refrigerated
Makes 2 cups

8 ripe plum tomatoes, cubed and seeded	½ jalapeño chile, minced, or more to taste
½ cup chopped sweet onion	2 tablespoons olive oil
⅓ cup chopped cilantro	2 tablespoons lime juice
3 garlic cloves, minced	Salt to taste

Combine all the ingredients in a medium bowl. Toss well.

Variations: For Avocado Salsa, add ½ cup cubed avocado to the mixture. This salsa is best used the same day it is prepared.

Chunky Fresh Tomato Sauce

Preparation time: 20 to 25 minutes
Storage: 3 days refrigerated
Makes 3 cups

2 tablespoons extra-virgin olive oil	Salt and freshly ground pepper to taste
2 garlic cloves, minced	¼ cup chopped fresh basil or parsley
1 can (28 ounces) plum tomatoes	

In a large skillet over medium heat, heat the olive oil. Add the garlic and sauté for 1 minute. Add the tomatoes and cook the mixture, stirring occasionally, until most of the liquid is evaporated, 20 to 25 minutes. Stir in the salt, pepper, and basil and remove from the heat.

Polenta

If you cannot find instant polenta, or don't feel like spending the extra money on it, use this simple but more time-consuming recipe.

Preparation time: 20 to 25 minutes, plus cooling
Storage: 3 days refrigerated
Makes 1 loaf

6 cups water

1 teaspoon salt

$1\frac{1}{2}$ cups finely ground cornmeal

1. In a large saucepan over high heat, bring the water to a boil. Add the salt and polenta, stirring constantly so the polenta doesn't clump. Cook, stirring, until the polenta is thick, 15 to 20 minutes.

2. Pour the polenta into an oiled loaf pan. Let cool completely before slicing and grilling.

Pie Dough

You will probably never have to make your own pie crusts, since it is extremely easy to find them frozen. However, I offer the recipe here because it does have a better flavor than the packaged ones, which invariably use vegetable shortening instead of butter.

Preparation time: 20 minutes, plus chilling
Storage: 3 days refrigerated, 3 months frozen
Makes a 9-inch crust

1¼ cups all-purpose flour

½ teaspoon salt

½ cup (1 stick) chilled butter, cut into small pieces

2 to 3 tablespoons ice cold water

1. In a large bowl, mix the flour and salt. Using a pastry blender or 2 knives, cut the butter into the flour mixture until coarse crumbs form. Add the water, tossing with a fork, until a soft dough forms. Alternatively, pulse the ingredients in a food processor until coarse crumbs form. Form the dough into a disk, wrap it in plastic wrap, and chill it in the refrigerator for at least 1 hour.

2. On a lightly floured surface, using a lightly floured rolling pin, roll the dough into a 12-inch circle. Fit the dough into a 9-inch pie pan. Trim the excess dough, leaving a 1-inch overhang. Decoratively flute the edges. Wrap in plastic wrap and chill the dough in the refrigerator (or freeze) until needed.

Variations: Substitute part lard or vegetable shortening for the butter.

Pizza Dough

Pizza dough is really very easy to make if you have an electric mixer.

Preparation time: 15 minutes, plus rising
Storage: 3 days refrigerated, 6 months frozen
Makes enough for 1 large pizza

1 package active dry yeast

½ teaspoon sugar

1 cup warm water (105–115° F.)

2 tablespoons extra-virgin olive oil

½ teaspoon salt

2 to 2½ cups all-purpose flour

1. In a small bowl, dissolve the yeast and sugar in the warm water. Let stand until foamy, 5 to 10 minutes.

2. Using a heavy-duty electric mixer fitted with the paddle attachment and set on low speed, mix the yeast mixture, olive oil, and salt. Add the flour, a little at a time, until the dough comes away from the sides of the bowl.

3. Turn out the dough onto a lightly floured surface. Knead until smooth and elastic, about 5 minutes, adding more flour as needed to prevent it from sticking. Place dough in a large greased bowl, turning to coat. Cover loosely with a damp cloth and let rise in a warm place until doubled in bulk, about 1 hour.

4. Punch the dough down and wrap in plastic. It can now be refrigerated or frozen until needed.

Variations: Substitute ½ cup cornmeal, buckwheat flour, rye flour, or whole-wheat flour for some of the all-purpose flour. Add a few tablespoons chopped fresh herbs, such as basil, thyme, parsley, tarragon, or a combination. Spinach and watercress are nice, too.

index